BEYOND SAFE PLACES

BEYOND SAFE PLACES

Trusting God through Life's Risks

RUTH SENTER

Harold Shaw Publishers
Wheaton, Illinois

ISBN 0-87788-084-0

Cover design by David LaPlaca

Cover photo © 1992 by Ron Thomas, FPG International Corp.

Library of Congress Cataloging-in-Publication Data

Senter, Ruth Hollinger, 1944-
    Beyond safe places : trusting God through life's risks / Ruth
Senter.
        p.   cm.
    Rev. ed of: Beyond safe places and easy answers. 1987
    ISBN 0-87788-084-0
    1. Women—Conduct of life.   2. Women—Religious life.
3. Senter, Ruth Hollinger, 1944-   . I. Senter, Ruth Hollinger,
1944-   Beyond safe places and easy answers. II. Title
BJ1610.S43 1992
248.8'43—dc20   92-23899
                                                 CIP

---

99 98 97 96 95 94 93

10 9 8 7 6 5 4 3 2

To
Elam and Gertrude Hollinger, my parents,
who risked without knowing it;
they simply obeyed

CONTENTS

BEYOND SAFE PLACES

Trusting God through Life's Risks

PART ONE

RISK TAKING

Why Is It So Hard?

1

Angry Rivers and Little White Churches

Self-Protection

Civilization as my husband and I have known it is lost to this endless backdrop of sagebrush, cactus, and yucca. As we follow the trail into the heart of Central Mexico, all signs of human life disappear. Every now and then a buzzard floats the sky above us, in search of dead animal carcasses, but other than that, there is not even movement from the wild.

"Just stay in sight of the telegraph lines, eight hours south until you come to Moctezuma," the letter from the missionary had said. We had high hopes of reaching the village before dark, but now we aren't so sure we'll be able to do that.

I glance at the sky. At my best calculations, only a few hours of light are left to the day, and Moctezuma has to be at least three hours away. Meanwhile, the road has disappeared, submerged by black swirling waters of a river. We were warned about the rainy season and what it did to travel. Now we understand. We climb out of our two International Travelall Vans and stare down at our formidable foe as it rages through the desolation.

We have traveled less than sixty miles in eight hours, down an unpredictable trail of sand, mud, rocks, ruts, holes, and water. So far we have found a way through the obstacles by using shovels, ropes, and six strong locals who appeared out of nowhere and volunteered to use their mule to pull us out of the mud. Now we face the river, and there is not a mule, rope, or local in sight. We are left to our own resources—a bunch of naive Illinoisans whose interaction with the wild has been little more than watching the seasons pass from inside thermostatically controlled houses.

Mexicans know not to fool around with swollen rivers. They are much wiser than that. They simply pull their tractors, trucks, or horses off the road and wait for the waters to recede. So what if the wait is a day or two? There is always mañana.

My body is damp with the afternoon's 100-degree-plus heat, and dust hangs in the air like fog sits in a harbor. The glamour of a trip to Mexico with fifteen high schoolers has long since worn off. In fact, it faded at the border when one of our fifteen couldn't find his passport.

"I might have packed it in my suitcase, and my suitcase is tied on top of the other van," someone had yelled from the back seat as the customs agent surveyed the scene of internal van chaos. He hastily counted heads and shuffled the passports. Fortunately, he didn't understand English and didn't take great care when counting heads. I didn't breathe deeply until we were well across the border and heading in a cloud of dust through the hovels of Agua Prieta, in search of telegraph lines going south.

A misplaced passport seems like a minor obstacle now as I look into the black waters before me. Mark, my husband, wades into the river to estimate depth and flow. He comes dripping up from the water's edge and heads toward his van. "I think we can make it. Keep her in first gear."

I feel like a shrinking soldier facing combat. I am the driver of the second van, and we must cross the river. We have come too far to turn back. But I want to go back, all the way back, maybe even to my mother's womb. I do not like rivers that pull your power from you and reduce you to marshmallow. I am not comfortable when life strips me of my ability to protect myself and leaves me vulnerable and exposed to peril. At the moment, I have no desire to risk, only the desire to run.

Mark is wrong. Crossing this river is not okay. There's too much at stake. Who are we to think we can navigate a furious river from the inside of an International Travelall? My head is full of swirling waters and anger toward Mark. *He doesn't care. He wants me to take my life into my own hands, not to speak of the kids we are responsible for, and drive through that river.* I can already see the headlines in the morning's *Chicago Tribune,* "Mexican river sweeps van load of teens to their death." I close my eyes in fear. I cannot go on. . . .

———————————— 🦎 ————————————

At another river, another time, and another place, my

dad was in the driver's seat, and the 1945 Chevy panel truck crawled over the muddy ruts, cutting through the woods toward Burnt Corn Creek and the Easel community. That small cluster of families had said to my dad, the preacher, "Come on over here and start a church for us, too."

On warm sunny days the road to the Easel community was picturesque with its red clay banks, towering white pines, and sprawling pin oaks—a brilliant display of nature at its best. That night, the display was drenched in darkness, and a downpour of rain pounded on the truck's roof like a tinsmith pounding tin. The trees cast shadows that appeared menacing to a six-year-old. *If only we didn't have to cross Burnt Corn Bridge,* I thought.

I shivered in the dark and moved closer to Bertha, who always felt like a second mother to me. Whenever we visited her, she hugged and kissed me and treated me like one of her own children. I felt some small security in being crammed into the middle of a press of bodies: Eubedean, with her hair tied up in a red bandana; Audrey, who was a high-school senior and sometimes let me wear her ruby-stoned class ring on my thumb; Christine, whose long dark hair fell along her shoulders in a perfect roll; Robert Earl, who knew more gospel songs than could fit in a songbook; Doug; Ola; Dorothy; and J. T. We were all on our way to Bible school, and they were my comfort.

I felt Daddy shift the truck into low gear, and I knew we had arrived at the top of the long, steep hill that led onto Burnt Corn Bridge. Even on clear days, the bridge was a six-year-old's nightmare—no guardrails, only loose boards that had little connection to anything. Now we had mud and rain to contend with. I closed my eyes, even though I didn't need to. Inside and out, there was nothing but blackness. Even the tiny comforting light from the dashboard was cut off by the bodies in front of me.

I felt the slide begin. The rear of the truck pulled away as though trying to disconnect itself. The rain pounded louder than ever, and I reached out in the dark for Bertha's hand. I knew the bridge was at the bottom of the slide, and I waited in agony.

Suddenly, Daddy cut the motor. We were sideways on the road. The headlights put out enough light to show us our dilemma. The bridge had disappeared. It was there, but underwater. We had driven this route enough times during the rainy season to know that when Burnt Corn Creek was on the rampage, it simply climbed its banks and took over the bridge. The only thing to do was to stop near the top of the hill, look down over the mud slide, figure how fast the creek was flowing, and calculate the risk.

Most people decided it wasn't worth it. They really didn't need to get to the Easel community after all. But when you were one of the few preachers for miles around and you had come to that remote section of southern Alabama to start churches and preach the gospel, you thought twice about turning back. Besides, people were waiting on the other side of the creek, under the big green army surplus tent, for the third night of the two-week evening Bible school to begin. When you were the preacher, your tent was the only church they had; your wooden folding chairs, their only pews; and your paperback gospel songbooks, their only hymnals. You didn't turn back.

I heard Daddy's voice through the dark, strong and confident. "Doug has checked out the water. He thinks we can make it. We'll be okay. Everyone sit still." If Doug and Daddy said it was okay, I felt it would be okay. Doug, often

Daddy's right-hand man, was young, tall, and tough. He knew the woods and every bump in the road. Certainly, he could tell whether the bridge was safe or not.

The engine started, the rear of the Chevy lined back up with the front, and we inched our way downward, forward, and onto Burnt Corn Bridge. I heard the waters and knew we were surrounded. Suddenly, the engine sputtered, gave a shudder, and died. It could not be revived. I shuddered with it and tried not to think about the dark waters around us and below.

My dad's voice remained calm. "How long will it take you to run home for your tractor?" he asked Doug.

"Not long, Preacher." A few more words—"Be back soon. Y'all sit tight"—and Doug was already climbing out the back of the truck and heading for home, three miles away.

We were left to the dark, the rain, and Burnt Corn Bridge without any sides. No one moved. At first no one talked, but soon Robert Earl started to sing, "Do Lord, oh do Lord, oh do remember me . . ." We all joined in. One song led to another, and before long we heard the tractor coming down the hill.

Once we were safely off the bridge with the help of Doug's tractor, the motor revived, and someone suggested another route to Bible school. An hour later we pulled into the grassy area beside the lighted tent. The rain was still pounding, but under the tent all was dry and the people were waiting, as though they'd had no doubt that the preacher would make it through.

Today if you follow the ravine where Burnt Corn Creek used to flow, you will find a little white church at the top of the hill, surrounded by pin oaks and pines. A few hundred feet to the right of the church, simple gravestone markings remind you of the passage of time. On a Sunday morning you can hear hymns drifting through the open windows. The attendance board is on the front right wall, next to the pulpit: "Number in Attendance Last Sunday: 45." Even if you forgot your fried chicken and butter beans, you are welcome to stay for dinner on the grounds. You may gather outside around the long wooden boards, nailed between two trees, which serve as a table and have stood for years as a symbol of community.

If it happens to be the thirtieth anniversary homecoming Sunday for the little white church, you will hear the sermon and recognize the voice of the preacher who calmed a truckload of frightened people on a dark night in the middle of a flooded creek. He has returned home for this one Sunday to share the rewards of risk and to give thanks for what can happen when obedience is more important than safety. . . .

―――――――――――――――― 🐿 ――――――――――――――――

But today I do not see rewards. I see only obstacles. I am not born to risk. I am born to protect myself, my loved ones, my reputation, and my valuables. In my need to protect, I am inclined to turn back, to avoid the peril completely. Why put myself in jeopardy when there are easier ways?

I feel safer if I keep my children close by. If I have a choice, I will not drive unknown mountain roads in the fog or walk the neighborhood alone after dark. Sometimes I choose psychological safety as well. I am inclined to let someone else knock on my neighbor's door and invite her to a Bible study. Rejection from a neighbor is scary business. I would rather swim laps at the neighborhood pool than join my husband, Mark, for a game of tennis because I know I can win at swimming laps by myself. Consistently coming in second is a risk I'd rather not have to take.

But God's call to me, His child, is not to safeness but always to something more—always upward, higher, further along. To by-pass the call is to settle for mediocrity, complacency, and dormancy. And should I choose not to risk, I will more than likely wake up some morning with the haunting question on my mind, "Could God have had something more for me, if only I had dared to trust?"

What, then, is this journey I must take—this venture into risk? It is, first of all, a venture into trust. Is God really God, able to take His crumbling, cowardly, disciple Peter and make of him a rock? Can He do the same for me if I give Him the chance? Is it possible for me to take up my pen with the apostle Paul and write confidently to the Christians in Ephesus, "Now to Him who is able to do exceedingly abundantly above all that [I] ask or think, according to the power that works in [me], to Him be glory . . . throughout all ages. . . . Amen" (Eph. 3:20–21)? Is there some exceeding abundance waiting for me if I will just step out of my safety zones and dare to trust?

Today as I stand by this Mexican river, I am struggling to protect my safety and the safety of those I care about and am responsible for. But perhaps, in a deeper way, I am protecting my reputation: Ruth Senter—wise decision maker and leader of teens. What will the parents think when their children go home and tell this story? Will the missionaries think it an unnecessary or irresponsible risk?

How might my need to protect affect others? It may rob a missionary family of three weeks of physical labor supplied by the group, a Mexican village of Bible school and Christian films in the evenings. It may keep seventeen individuals from experiencing the rewards of service to people of another culture.

The journey to risk is also the journey toward courage. If I would know courage, I must stand with Peter the coward in the middle of a boat being tossed by the winds. I must be willing to be terrified for a while as I look across the waves and see the ghostlike figure coming toward me. I must make irrational moves—call out some foolish proposal, "Lord, if it's You, tell me to come to You on the water."

If I would know risk, I must obey in fear and trembling. I must climb over the side of the boat and let myself down onto nothing but pure trust in the power of God. If I would know risk, I must be willing to fail for a while—to be nearly undone by the wind and the waves, to hear the strong indictment, "Why did you doubt?" and as I climb dripping wet back into the safety of the boat, to see the looks of amusement on my companions' faces as they think: *Silly Peter. Who does he think he is?*

I have doubted, yes. I have failed. But I have taken the leap and found God reliable. His hand is always reaching down to me in my risk—rescuing me from a watery grave, calming the storm, climbing back into the boat with me. Still shaking, fear now turned to exhilaration, I bow low in worship and proclaim, "Truly You are the Son of God" (see Matt. 14:25–33). For in the end, risk always points me away from myself and faces me squarely into the power of almighty God.

But the journey of risk does not end with getting out of the boat. It begins there. It goes from a stormy lake to the halls of the high priest in Jerusalem, where Peter and John stand, newly released from their prison cell. I must stand there with them, before a hostile crowd—high priest Annas, Caiaphas, John, Alexander, other members of the high priest's family, the elders, and the teachers of law. They have silenced Jesus but do not know what to do about men who have influenced nearly five thousand inhabitants of Jerusalem in the direction of Jesus of Nazareth, Son of God.

My voice must echo with that of Peter through the religious court, "Nor is there salvation in any other, for there is no other name under heaven given among men by which we must be saved." The jurors are silenced in awe. They scribble on their legal pads: ordinary men with extraordinary courage, suspects who have obviously been with Jesus. They huddle in caucus. "What are we going to do with these men? Everybody living in Jerusalem knows they have done an outstanding miracle."

Courage cannot be contained. Peter and John walk from the hall in freedom because the Sanhedrin see all the people praising and glorifying God for what happened (see Acts 4:12–21). For one night, in a little fishing boat on Lake Gennesaret, courage was born, courage that astounded the religious supreme court, added to the church five thousand men, began momentum for the greatest movement the world has ever known—the advancement of the good news about Jesus Christ, Son of God. Risk took the coward Peter and made of him a rock.

I stand at this angry Mexican river involved in a terrifying moment of choice.

"Lord, if it's You, tell me to come."

There are no safety clauses, no emergency plans, no guarantees, only a simple, direct, "Come."

I climb into the driver's seat of the International Travelall, start the ignition, and follow Mark's van as its tail-lights disappear beneath the torrent. I feel the movement of water around me, the shifting of the river's bottom under my wheels. I have risked not carelessly, but obediently. And now I find a hand reaching down to me in my risk. We cross the river in terror, but we cross the river. Three more hours and we see the twinkling lights of Moctezuma in the distance. We find a man in the town square who speaks English and guides us safely to the missionary's home.

Today, some twenty years later, a young woman works beside her husband in the interior of Mexico, teaching the message of love. She was one of the passengers in the International Travelall. Now and then the thought comes to me, *Would Linda be in Mexico today as a missionary had we never crossed the river?* Only the Keeper of the divine blueprint knows for sure, but in my continuing struggle to risk, I look back to that angry Mexican river and am glad that I found the courage to go into the swirling waters.

2

Strange Shadows on the Wall

The Need to See and Know

During one of the empty hours between midnight and dawn, when the world seems exaggerated and distorted, I am awakened by a strange sensation—internal pressure of a kind I have never felt before. I know immediately it has nothing to do with the pizza and watermelon eaten earlier, even though someone at the party had suggested pizza was good for inducing labor. I look toward my alarm clock. It's just this side of 2:00 A.M.—an alien time zone for sound sleepers like me. The streetlight shadow on my wall, usually a friendly familiarity, is harsh and haunting tonight, disfigured like a monster mask at Halloween.

Looking into the darkness of the night is anything but reassuring. What lies ahead for me? What is this flutter of life within me, pushing so hard for emergence? What are the pains in my back? Tonight I feel I am a stranger to my own body, which is suddenly unpredictable and out of control.

The night moves on as I wait in shadow. Pain enters and exits in short little gaps. It's the pain of labor, yes, but also it's the pain of not knowing what lies ahead. In some ways, it's a greater pain. I can do something about labor. I have read the books, attended the classes, practiced breathing, and exercised faithfully every day. But the pain of not being able to see down the road—the risk of life without guarantees—stalks my bedroom.

What of the future? Will my baby be normal? Safe? Healthy? Happy? Where will she be sixteen years from now? Thirty-five? Fifty? Will she love and serve the God of her parents? Soon the doctors will cut the umbilical cord, my child will take on separateness, and I will relinquish control. Without control there are no guarantees. Tonight I stare into the dark for assurances. I find nothing but a strange shadow without and unknown pressure within.

I am trying to see in the dark, but I am not meant to see at night. Perhaps that's why I lie awake and wonder what to do. If it were day, I would feel more confident, more at peace. In my humanness I want to walk where I can see, avoiding the dark.

A part of me wants to stay in bed rather than risk the night, to sleep the blissful sleep of youth, where your mother covers you with a warm blanket when you are cold, where pain is cured by a pill, and tomorrow is always certain. In that pleasant, peaceful comfort zone, you look for assurances, and they are always there. You don't worry about yourself; someone else worries for you. You have no concerns for others; they are not your responsibility. Life maintains its equilibrium, and you are cushioned from jolts, like a baby in the womb, surrounded by embryonic fluid.

But this night the cushion is gone. I am on the raw edge of life where no one covers you with a blanket when you are cold and smoothes out your day before you. Where night and day are the same and you have to walk whether you see or not.

Mark turns on the bedroom light and goes to the front hall closet for my suitcase, which has been packed for days. I get dressed, then take one last look into the nursery with its freshly painted white furniture and its red-and-white wallpaper. The musical lamb smiles at me from between the bars of the crib. I wind him up and listen one more time to "Mary Had a Little Lamb." It's like saying good-bye to an old friend. This will be a different place when I return. I will be a different person. What will it be like? I don't know. What is this thing called parenthood? How does one survive without guarantees? I do not know the answers to these questions, but I must go to the hospital anyhow.

The nurse at the emergency entrance smiles and nods as Mark and I take a seat and I proceed to fill out the forms. She calls for an orderly and a wheelchair.

"Has my doctor arrived yet?" I am looking for familiarity. The nurse doesn't know and has no way of finding out at the moment. He will be here when it's time. She doesn't seem in a hurry, nor does she seem to sense a need to give me information.

"Which room?" the orderly asks. The nurse doesn't know that just yet, either. All labor rooms are presently full, but one should be available soon, she assures me. The orderly returns to the book he has been reading, while

Mark and I sit and count the minutes between contractions. The nurse is right; there is no hurry. But at least I would like to know the plan. Right now, there seems to be none with an orderly who is buried in his book, a nurse who pecks away at her typewriter, and a doctor who is nowhere to be seen.

It's time to turn on the lights. To walk by sight for a while. But the night is not over. In fact, each hour seems to bring more uncertainties. I am moved into an available bed in the labor room. My doctor arrives. He comes and goes every half-hour or so. The nurses move quietly and confidently around me. They are in and out of the room. The clock on the wall grinds slowly through the night and into the day. The pressure and pain increase, like a lead weight pulling me downward. I feel myself becoming the object of careful scrutiny. A monitor. X rays. Constant checks. Nurses change shifts. Now there are two doctors. I know and trust them both. They are gentle and kind, but they have no answers for me.

"Why no dilation?"

"Why the irregular heartbeat?"

"Why the close contractions but a baby that will not move?"

The doctor stands by my bed for the third time in an hour. He looks down at me with wrinkled brow. His voice is sober as he takes my hand and says, "I don't know about you, Ruth . . ." He waits. Then as though exploring one last possibility, he asks, "Do you know anything about your mother's first delivery?"

"Hard and long." It's all I say, and he doesn't ask for more. I know more. Much more about the pain of her first delivery. Nine months later she would be pregnant with me, her second child. I had often heard the story of my birth. . . .

----------------------------------- ⟨⟩ -----------------------------------

The year was 1944, and the world was at war. The Allies swarmed northern France in June of that year, and before it was all over, 16 million military men were dead. The papers at home painted the gory details, and one mother sat a continent away, reading the evening news. August 14, 1944. Finally, she could read no more; folding the paper, she peered into the hot darkness as it fell around the front porch swing where she sat. Out there somewhere a mother's child was dying, yet she knew hers was being born. She felt the muscles of her stomach, hard like a brick. In between contractions she listened for the quarter-hour chimes on the grandfather's clock that stood just inside the front door. They seemed an eternity apart. There was no stopping the tremors of birth that edged her toward the zero hour. Her child was about to be born. She sat and thought of the implications.

Her first delivery had been abnormal; some would say near tragic. Long labor. Ether. Forceps. Oxygen deficiency. She and her first-born would live with a lifetime of ramifications. Now her second child was due, and her country was at war. Would there be a lifetime of ramifications for this child, also? Would her second-born listen to bombs falling and air-raid sirens blaring instead of the peaceful night sounds of the crickets and the soft chime of the grandfather's clock? Would her son or daughter live off rationed food and black out the lights at dusk for fear of bomber attacks?

She could not dismiss the evening news. Its shadow lay heavy, as oppressive as the sultry August air that seemed to be squeezing breath from her. The irony: she was hostessing life while her nation courted death; officers a continent away strategized the taking of life while she agonized to give it. While warships rained shells on the German batteries, she sat on her front porch swing and prayed for the safety of her unborn child.

She wiped the perspiration from her forehead. Was it the dark she felt? The pain? The memory of an earlier delivery? The faraway quakes from a nation at war? The uncertainty of life and birth?

Yet life could not be stopped. It would come when it would come, and it would be what it would be. It would come suddenly, and she would be helpless, except to breathe deep and bear down. Nature and war would have their way.

She opened the screen door and tiptoed in to waken her sleeping husband. She was ready, even though the world wasn't. But then, the world would never be ready to promise safety and security for her children. The world would never hand her the blueprint ahead of time. If she would walk, she must walk by faith, not by sight.

Although it was time to go, there remained one thing to do. She paused in the darkened room, and as the grandfather's clock ticked above her, she knelt by the couch and gave her unborn baby back to God. She made a commitment to a walk in the dark—war, pain, notwithstanding—to trust God with what she could not see and did not know. Her choice was simple. She could tighten her grip on her unknown future—protect, control, manipulate, protest—or she could face life with an open hand—palm up, letting go of a child she could not keep for the love, joy, and peace she could not lose. She chose the latter. . . .

But I do not easily let go of life without guarantees. I cannot trust a world gone sour—doctors who make mistakes, people who hate and make wrong choices, influencers who lead astray, promoters who have only their own good at heart, and deteriorating conditions that set in with Eden's fall. I live in a world that calls for healthy cynicism, eagle-eye surveillance, quick-wittedness, and conditions spelled out beforehand—anything but a walk in the dark. The twentieth century requires sophistication, not some blind acquiescence. But the twentieth century also ties its people up in knots, hands them sleeping pills for the pressure by night and Valium for the pressure by day—end result of making oneself the creator of one's own destiny. On the other hand, risk agrees to the walk in the dark, lets go of what it cannot create or control, and therein finds its peace.

For the journey into risk is a venture into faith. I must keep walking at night, whether the moon shines brightly or not. I must keep believing in my child, whether I see returns for my trust or not. I must continue to articulate my convictions, whether anyone seems to understand or not. I must keep on praying, even when I seem to have nothing to show for my prayers. I must say out loud to myself, "Jesus loves me," even when I feel cut off from Him. I must post a sign in my mind—God Can Be Trusted—even when I am lying in a hospital bed wondering what is happening to me and to my unborn baby. For "faith is the substance of things hoped for, the evidence of things not seen" (Heb. 11:1). Faith is trust in the Keeper of the circumstances rather than trust in the circumstances themselves.

If I would know the freedom to risk, I must control my mind and replace worries about "what if . . ." with thoughts of "what is. . . ." I must curb my imagination rather than create tragic fiction with my life. I must think about the present instead of always trying to construct the future. I must ask God for daily bread, not a lifetime supply. I must call up memories of another time, in the past when I could not see the Promised Land but I could feel the promised One. I must say to myself, "This walk in the dark is worth it. I know from experience."

The venture into risk is also a venture into giving up. If I would know risk, I must stand along the marshy banks of the Nile River with my three-month-old son, Moses, in my arms. In my mind, I must see written across his round little face, "this child was Mine before he was yours." Pushing past the cattails and reeds that grow at the river's edge, I must look up into the sky and return this bone of my bone, flesh of my flesh, to his Maker. I must step into the muck and place my tiny bundle into the papyrus basket coated with tar and pitch. I must deposit myself in that basket, tear my own heart out of my body, and lay it in the crocodile-infested waters of the Nile River. I must take one final glance, give the basket a gentle shove, and stumble blindly back through the cattails and reeds.

But the journey of risk does not end with the basket floating in the river. It continues as Moses stands in Pharaoh's palace, first as an adopted child with all the privileges and then as an emissary of God pleading the fate of an entire nation. Risk takes Moses as leader, over the burning desert sands, across the barren plateaus with no food or water, always onward toward the Promised Land. He strikes a rock and brings forth a stream, holds a stick over the sea and stands the waves on end. The journey of risk leads him to a mountaintop, where he receives instruction for life that will be the blueprint for generations. And when the journey comes to the end, he receives a line in the obituary column of the morning newspaper that reads, "Since then there has not arisen in Israel a prophet like Moses, whom the LORD knew face to face, in all the signs and wonders which the LORD sent him to do in the land of Egypt . . . and by all that mighty power and all the great terror which Moses performed in the sight of all Israel" (Deut. 34:10–12). All this because one mother, on a sultry afternoon in Egypt, pushed through the cattails and dared to give her baby over to unknown circumstances, trusting the God behind the circumstances.

I now lie in this hospital labor room involved in my own moment of choice, a battle of my mind. Do I continue to dwell on my need for a normal, healthy child? To ask the questions and demand the answers? Or do I agree to this walk in the dark? Do I return with my mother, to the living room couch, and there give God the option? Do I deposit my child in a flimsy basket in the Nile River? Lord, it's asking more than I can give.

The moments continue to tick away on the clock; the monitor's beep drones on. I reach for another cup of ice, and Mark rearranges the blankets around my feet. When the doctors and nurses have gone, I take Mark's hand and ask him to pray with me the prayer of dedication. God can be trusted. Everything else is pure speculation.

Tonight, seventeen years later, I am still staring into darkness. I am waiting for our first-born, Jori, to return from a date. "Bye, Mom. See you around midnight," she had said hours earlier as she bounded out the door in her typical exuberance and zest for life. She is the type who honors her commitments, and I had no doubt that she would keep her word.

But my digital clock advances to 12:23, and there is no trace of Jori. I am back in the labor room, giving up my need for guarantees, handing over to God my child's safe-keeping, and asserting my confidence in the Holder of the blueprint. The walk of trust will never be my natural instinct. Tonight I would stare into the dark and create all kinds of tragic reasons for Jori's lateness, but the memory of a decision made years ago in a hospital labor room gives me courage now to trust when I cannot see. Instead of a gory crash by the side of the road, I try to visualize Psalm 23—the "still waters." For when all is said and done, all of life is a grope in the dark. Risk is simply deciding how I will respond to the grope. Jori arrives at 12:30 with an account of car trouble and no nearby phone to call. We have no doubts. I kiss her good-night, turn off the light, and sleep in peace.

3

The Chickens That Came to Lunch
Inhibitions

I am barely back from the delivery room when I begin creating motherhood in my mind. I create an awesome responsibility for myself: forever on call, forever the example, nurturer, teacher, friend. I am exhausted before I begin, and my dream tonight is not one of rest.

I am trapped in a long, empty hall. My footsteps bounce off the walls like an echo between two hills. I look for a way out, but the doors have no handles. The exit signs are blank frames. The windows are shuttered and barred. But I must get out. I must find my baby. She has fallen into a swimming pool, and no one sees her. She screams with hunger, and the food is locked behind iron doors. I cannot get to the food or the swimming pool.

I awaken tired and realize I have been sleeping the sleep

that comes after having given birth. It is also the sleep of responsibility—a working sleep. I wonder if all my nights from now on will be working nights followed by working days. Working to maintain the life of this tiny stranger I do not yet know, to build a relationship with this person wrapped in pink, to be the mother I think I should be, and to be the mother I think "they" think I should be. (Who "they" are, I have no idea.)

The rosebuds on my night stand are beginning to open, and outside my window, white clouds skim the bright June sky like sailboats at sea, but I don't pay much attention. I cannot get beyond thoughts of myself and my responsibility. I must be a good mother. I hear myself sigh, and the nurse asks if something hurts somewhere.

How do I tell her that the hurt is in my mind, that it comes from caring so much, from wanting to do it all right? How can I tell her that I sigh because the umbilical cord has been broken? Or maybe I sigh because the umbilical cord has not been broken. I don't know why I sigh, but I do. The nurse pats my arm, then kneads my empty stomach. We are both involved in the process of afterbirth.

I look at my flat stomach—a reminder that Nature, the automatic caretaker of my baby for nine months, has relieved itself of responsibility and transferred its charge to me. Like the curator of a museum, I will spend my days guarding a treasure; the only difference is that this treasure can walk away and say no and play in the dirt. The nurse sticks a thermometer into my mouth, and I stretch out my arm for the blood-pressure cuff. If only the pressure in my mind could be so easily cared for.

A baby cries somewhere down the hall, and I wonder if it's mine. The screaming bundle of pink rolls into my room, and I go down my mental list. Hunger? Wet bottom? Diaper pins? Diaper rash? Her screams continue, and the pressure mounts to fix it. What must I fix? I do not know. I feed her and hold her close, next to my stomach, with legs tucked up under her in her prenatal position. But she is still unsettled. She has fallen into the pool and I am trying desperately to rescue her, but I can't get to her. I relive my dreams even as I ring for the nurse.

"Honey, she's okay. She's just exercising her lungs. Babies cry, you know." But I try to fix it anyhow. I am her mother. I must spare her from pain, stomach cramps, indigestion, or whatever. I rock. I sing. Finally, we walk. We are passing the nurses' station when my legs lose their strength. The hall begins to rotate, and I move toward the wall for support.

"Don't rush it, honey," a nurse says as she reaches for my screaming baby and guides me back to bed. "You're still pretty weak."

But in my mind I am strong. I must be strong to be the mother I want to be. The thought hangs over me, sapping energy and draining my spirit.

Later in the evening Mark arrives for visiting hours. We walk to the nursery to check on Jori. We know she is well cared for; mostly we make the trip to the nursery for pride. We stand at the window and marvel at her beauty. She sleeps peacefully now. One finger points straight up over the edge of the blanket, and every now and then, the muscles around her mouth twitch so they look like smiles. Bone of my bone. Flesh of my flesh. Yesterday, a part of my body. Tonight, more a part of my heart. I want for her all the peace and contentment life can possibly hold. And I feel the responsibility to make it happen for her.

We are still looking into the antiseptic white nursery

when the aroma of barns and animals passes behind us. I am alerted immediately. That smell doesn't belong here. Nurseries are germ free. How did animal odors get by the woman in pink at the front desk?

The young couple heads down the hall toward the sunroom. I'm relieved they don't stop at the nursery. Even though all I can see is their backs, they are a strange combination. His cowboy boots are cracked, and clods of dirt still cling to the soles. I notice his patched jeans and dirty fingernails as he puts his arm around the girl at his side and reaches to open the door. Her body looks frail, and she wears nothing but a hospital gown that gaps open in the back. I wonder what has happened to modesty. What are they doing on the maternity floor?

"There goes a story," I say casually to Mark. I have no intentions of finding out about them. I am too preoccupied with my own responsibilities right now. Other times I would have probably followed my curiosity. At least I would have asked their names. Tonight I don't even care.

Whether I care or not, I learn their names from Mark the next afternoon. I shouldn't be surprised that he has made contact with them. He does so as a minister and also as a person who genuinely enjoys meeting new people.

"I met Sam, the young man in the cowboy boots, last night as I was leaving," he tells me, dropping the mail on my night stand. "Their baby girl was born premature an hour before Jori. She lived two hours. He's a horsewalker, from over on the backside, behind the racetrack. I took him home last night because they don't own a car. He hitchhikes back and forth to the hospital. Ellie's only sixteen and devastated that she doesn't have a baby to take home. When we got to their trailer, he invited me in for coffee. We sat and talked 'til eleven."

My smugness about dirty fingernails and barn odors starts to wane. I think of my own bundle of pink in the nursery. Day after tomorrow we will go home together. But I also think about Mark's roaming the backside of the racetrack in the middle of the night. The horse-racing crew is a tough lot. Almost every month the paper contains stories about some sort of rumblings out behind the tracks, once even a murder.

But rumblings and murders are the furthest things from Mark's mind. "They don't have insurance or money, and the hospital won't release her until they pay their bill. I was able to get money from the fellowship fund at church . . . took the check by this morning. You should have seen the look on his face. They'll be out of here this afternoon. It's not good for her to be around the babies."

I enjoy Mark's enthusiasm for ministry and care giving, and I am glad, too, for the sake of the sixteen-year-old. I assume the horsewalker and his wife are a closed chapter, but just after Jori has been taken back to the nursery, Ellie appears at my door. Her blonde hair hangs loose and unkempt around her face, and the dark circles under her eyes give her a hollow look, as if she has not slept for days. She is still wearing the blue-and-white hospital gown, and I suspect it's still gapping in the back.

"You and your husband sure have been good to us."

Thinking she is going to cry, I motion her in, but she hangs onto the doorframe. I am feeling a bit of guilt about the "you" in her sentence. I haven't given her more than five minutes of thought.

She continues, "You have a baby girl, I heard. We're leaving this afternoon, but would you bring your baby by to see us sometime soon? Your husband knows where we live . . . third trailer on the right, row eight. I'd sure like to hold your baby." Her words are more of a plea than an invitation, and as though she is afraid I might say no, she gives a faint wave and is gone before I have time to respond.

My mind game takes over again. Take my baby to the backside? I don't even want to go near there myself. Row upon row of tiny trailers, packed into dust and dirt. No grass, no trees, no wide two-car garages; just trailers and barns and flies and the smell of horses. On days when the wind blows a certain direction, we have both the flies and the horse smell in our back yard, which is only three miles away. But take my baby deliberately into the dirt and smells? Newborns have not yet built their immunities. We don't even know the people. What if it's a trap? I've heard of grieving mothers who are so desperate they kidnap babies right out of hospital nurseries.

I cannot take my baby into the backside. My sense of responsibility has become my inhibitor, and I am not free to venture into the dirt and germs of an unknown place and people. At this point, to protect is more important than to trust. I am a mother, in charge of a new baby. . . .

But I was once a child of four with pigtails and blue ribbons and smocked dresses. My T-strap brown shoes were always polished and my white lace socks folded over in perfect alignment. Mother always saw to it.

During the day, I ran with the wild, through the woods, after the dogs, my older brother, Jimmie, and the kids down the road. We climbed fences, built our forts out of firewood logs, and dug our tunnels into red clay banks. But when I came in, I was a lady again. Mother rebraided my hair, and I scrubbed under my fingernails until the skin was nearly raw. Or I would climb into the rubber army surplus bathtub that Mother had filled with hot water from a big pan on the stove. She set it up for baths in the corner of the garage, and when we were finished, she folded it up and put it away. I liked to soak in suds and feel clean. Mother always commented on how good I smelled after a bath.

One day I did not soak in suds but rode through the dust toward the Sandwell community. Lola Blackwell, along with her husband and eight kids, had invited us for dinner. They attended our church and lived in the woods beside a creek. The dirt road was filled with ruts and bounced our Country Squire station wagon up and down like a rubber ball. I didn't worry about the vibrations for myself, but I was concerned about my new baby brother, Denny, who slept in the back of the car, oblivious to one of his first ventures into the outside world. I wondered what the washboard road was doing to his formula, but Mother didn't seem worried. She chatted happily with Daddy in the front seat.

I wondered, too, what the white lace bassinet cover would look like by the time we got home. I was surprised Mother had brought it, it was so lovely and clean. I reached back and touched the delicate lace. Denny slept peacefully while the dust flew outside and the car vibrated over the ruts.

The Blackwells—all ten of them—were glad to see us. They raced toward the car before we'd even come to a complete stop. For them, our station wagon was novel enough—few people in those parts of the woods drove a car, much less a station wagon—but we had a new baby, too. Mama Blackwell immediately reached into the basket for Denny.

I noticed that her front tooth was missing, and I hoped the wad of tobacco she was chewing wouldn't drip through the gap where her tooth should have been. Denny had on his very best new blue outfit, a present from relatives back East. Mama Blackwell must have noticed the new outfit, because she aimed her spit well enough out into the air so it missed the blue cotton suit. The tobacco juice made little dirt rivulets where it landed on the ground, and the hound dogs came to see if it was food.

"Sure is mighty good of y'all to come to dinner today. I told Emerson I just couldn't bear to have Sonny leave for the army without having the preacher to dinner just one more time. I think you-all do him some good. Now . . . y'all come in . . . come in."

"May, shoo those chickens off the porch so the preacher there can have a seat. I think I might just keep me this here baby. Sure is a sweet one, just like his mama I reckon."

She beamed at my mother who placed the white lace bassinet in the middle of the chickens. They still hadn't moved from the porch, despite May's swish of an old rag, or maybe it was the dishcloth she was swishing, I couldn't tell.

"Y'all have a seat." She offered Mother the one ladder-back chair that leaned against the wall.

Mother placed it carefully on all four legs so they missed the cracks in the floor. The chickens scratched underneath the chair, and the hogs rooted in mud just beyond the kitchen door.

May turned her swatting rag from the chickens to the flies, which had already discovered Denny. One sat on his closed eyelid, but Mother didn't even notice. She was too busy complimenting Mama Blackwell on her lovely gourd planters and morning-glory vines. Daddy took a seat among the hound dogs on the top porch step, and the children passed my baby brother around like he was a little rag doll.

"Careful now of that there baby. . . ," Mama Blackwell warned, but other than that she didn't seem any more concerned than my mother was. Mama Blackwell never once asked if the children had washed their hands. I noticed how black their fingernails were, but then my fingernails would probably be black, too, if I had to carry the wash water up from the creek.

We sat on the porch for a while, and then Mama Blackwell announced dinner. The children, still with unwashed hands, lined up on the backless benches while the adults pulled up the only four chairs in the house (counting the one brought in from the porch). Daddy said grace, and all fourteen of us pronounced the "Amen" together. We turned our plates over and dug into the collard greens, chicken and dumplings, and black-eyed peas. We had to move fast to keep the flies off our food. The Blackwell kids knew how to shoot the flies off the rim of their iced tea glasses like they were shooting marbles in a game. Jimmie and I were new to the game, so we missed most of the flies we aimed for. Almost by instinct, I did wipe the rim of my glass each time I drank.

When baby Denny started to cry, Mama Blackwell jumped up to make him some sugar water. "Good for new babies' digestion," she said as she used one hand to pour water from the tin dipper into the bottle and the other hand to bounce Denny up and down. A little sugar, and the bottle was ready. Mama Blackwell didn't bother to heat it. Most of the wood had burned down in the stove anyway. Besides the day was warm enough. Denny stopped crying the minute the bottle touched his lips. Mama Blackwell propped the bottle up with her chin, shooed the flies off her biscuit with one hand, and popped it into her mouth with the other.

"These have to be the best biscuits I've ever eaten," my mother said to Mama Blackwell as she neatly spread the second half of her biscuit with fresh blueberry jam. "The self-rising flour does make a difference, doesn't it? I should take lessons from you." Mama Blackwell looked pleased.

I reached for my piece of banana pie and refilled my glass with iced tea. Then I sat back and gave a long satisfied sigh. The gentle November air blew through the windows, the doors, and the cracks in the walls.

It was nice to be in such a pleasant place with the blue sky coming in through the cracks and the sound of chickens scratching on the boards, looking under the table for food. Daddy and Mr. Blackwell talked about the poor cotton crop of the year, and Mother asked Sonny about his plans for the army. Mama Blackwell tossed a few chicken bones to the dogs, and we knew dinner was officially over since throwing the scraps to the dogs was the unspoken benediction.

I gave my brother a little kiss on the top of his head as I headed toward the door with Jimmie and the Blackwell children. We ran through the mud toward the barn, and I noticed red clay sticking to the bottoms of my brown T-straps. I had polished them just before we came. I looked back toward the house. Mother was helping to scrape the plates and wasn't even looking after us. Even if she had been, I was sure it wouldn't matter to her if I did get my shoes muddy.

I ran happily on with the pack, my brown braids flying

behind me, and my arms opened wide to the warm fall sunshine. I would polish my shoes again when I got home. And I even forgot about the rattlesnake Mr. Blackwell told us about over dinner, the one he had killed yesterday by the corncrib. I was free—to run through the mud, climb in the corncrib, splash in the creek, and roll down the hill in rubber tractor tires. No hesitations. No inward restraints. No inhibitions or preoccupations with safety, either psychological or physical. My mother was free, and so was I. . . .

––––––––––––––––– 🐓 –––––––––––––––––

But here in this bright hospital room, having just given birth to my first-born, I struggle with the restraints of my mind. Doing a good job seems more important than partaking of the moment; thoughts of myself and my child, more important than thoughts of others. Snagged on the internal pressures I have stacked up for myself, I am not free to enjoy the roses blooming by my bed or reach out to a needy sixteen-year-old down the hall.

Most of my restraints come from the lists I make for myself, expectations of myself, critiques of my performances, worries over what others are thinking, and fear for my safety. Inhibitions come, and like thieves tying up their victims, they keep me from thinking about the world beyond myself. I become slave to responsibility, reputation, evaluation, cleanliness, and safety.

But God calls me, His child, not to restraints of the mind but to freedom of the spirit. By-passing the call means I will cautiously tiptoe my way through life, afraid of awakening adventure and surprise. And one morning I will open my eyes and realize to my dismay that I have not only tied myself up in a hopeless web but also passed my inhibitions along to my children.

What, then, is the risk I must take when it comes to my inhibitions? If I would know risk, I must rid myself of my mind games, free myself from myself. I must monitor my thoughts: thoughts of myself versus thoughts of others. I must relax in my intensities. Laugh at myself. Smell my roses. Play "Monopoly." Focus on the world: birds singing in the crab apple tree, the president signing papers in the White House, a merchant selling Turkish carpets in a stall on the streets of Istanbul—all things, places, and people over whom I have no control and for whom I have no responsibility.

If I would know risk, I must reach across my sense of appropriateness and embrace those who are different from myself. I must eat where the chickens scratch under the table, go to the racetrack backside where life gets rough now and then, and run through the mud even when I prefer polished shoes and bubble bath. I must see need as more important than protocol, the person as more important than the person's style.

If I would know risk, I must push through the crowd with Jesus on my way to the home of Jairus, a ruler of the synagogue (see Mark 5:22–34). In the northern lake country, the air around Capernaum hangs heavy. I must breathe the sultry air and smell the press of sweaty bodies around me, reaching toward me in their need. Someone pulls the tassel of my outer garment. I must acknowledge the touch. But it's the touch of defilement. She is a woman. By Levitical law, religious leaders do not even look on a woman, much less allow a woman to touch them. She is also an unclean woman, having lived with a bloody discharge for twelve years.

But need must always be more important than cleanliness. I must take the leap—forget the odor, the disease, and the risk of physical and religious contamination. I must stop in my tracks and touch society where it bleeds, Levitical law or not. On this hot Galilean afternoon, I must also move beyond my need to have everyone understand or approve. I must look on the outcast with love, call her "daughter," and affirm her for her faith, even though the religious leaders are standing nearby. If I would know risk, I must be prepared to lay aside my conformity.

June is soft, the night gentle, as Mark and I turn through the gates into the backside, three weeks after Jori's birth. She is asleep in my arms. We have brought ice cream and cookies. There are no phones in these forgotten trailer islands, so we could not call to tell them we were coming. Mark remembers the way, since he was here only a few weeks ago.

The lights from the inside of the trailers appear dim, almost as though they don't want outsiders to violate their turf. Children play in the dusky lanes, and men sit on their trailer steps and talk. We drive to row eight, third trailer on the right. Two little girls are jumping rope in the dust. Mark knocks on the screen door. A man with a beer can in his hand and what looks to be about three days' growth of beard on his face shuffles forward.

"We're looking for Sam and Ellie. They used to live here."

He hardly waits for Mark to finish his sentence.

"Cleared out last week. Gone away. Don't know where."

Mark returns to the car, and we drive silently back through the gates. Ellie will never hold my baby. I feel a sense of loss.

And today, years removed from the backside, I drive toward a speaking engagement at a tiny church on Chicago's near South Side. Riddled with a reputation for unrest, this neighborhood is an unknown neighborhood to me. My map is carefully spread out on the seat beside me. I exit the Eisenhower Expressway, lock all four car doors, and pray for green lights.

Me? Driving alone on Chicago's near South Side? I would not have always done so, but somehow, woven into my memories, is a sixteen-year-old, would-be mother, who never got to hold my baby. Perhaps it is that memory that pushes me toward the South Side when I would rather sit safely in the suburbs. For risk is not risk until it can trust enough to move beyond its natural inhibitions.

4

Would Someone Please Take the Gun Away?
Fear

I drive under a Dutch elm canopy of green. Today the trees provide cool shade from the summer's heat. Of the twelve elms on our street, two are already gone, victims of Dutch elm disease. I spot two more orange x's on the tree trunks and know that it will be just a matter of time before more trees are reduced to stumps by the city street department. Today, though, they line the driveway, ready to welcome me home, and for some reason, I seem to need their support, even if it's just by way of shade.

We turn into the driveway of the two-story brick parsonage that has been home for the last few years, compliments of the church for Mark's ministry to youth. I glance into my rearview mirror. My two towheads, Jori and Nicky, are nodding in the back seat. At least they've gotten their afternoon naps. It's a good day for digging in the sandbox, running in the grass, or weeding in the garden. The gladioluses are in full bloom now, and I need to pull the rhubarb before it gets too thick and tough. I pause in satisfaction at simple summer pleasures. For a moment I forget that Dutch elm disease is gobbling up our shade.

I have just turned off the motor when around the corner of the garage, into the middle of my simple summer pleasures, walks a figure who might have come from the pages of some hard rock magazine. His long black hair is kept out of his face by a red headband, and a large gold serpent hangs from a chain against his chest. He does not wear a shirt, and his cigarette falls out of his mouth as he starts to speak. I notice immediately that he is swaying in the breeze.

"Hi, Ruth. Remember me?" His words are thick, his eyes glazed.

My mind is digging for the missing information. If only I can call him by name, perhaps the threat will be over. I glance back at the kids, step out of the car, and raise my five-foot-five-and-a-half-inch frame as tall as it will go.

"May I help you with something?" I think I'm brave, but at this moment I'm not sure. Most neighbors are not yet home from work, and Mark has gone to the city for the afternoon. There's not a sound or a movement on the entire street. Except for my two small children, I'm alone with this stranger who knows my name.

"Is Mark around?" He takes a step toward me. "You still don't know me, do you?" His grin seems more like a jeer. He attempts to tell me how hard it has been to track us down, but mostly I hear a string of profanities. He is still grinning at me as he lights another cigarette.

Then as though information has been frozen by my fear

and suddenly thawed, I recognize Steve, one of our youth group members from a former church. He was thinner then. Clean-cut. Minus the gold serpent and the three large tattoos that decorate his forearms. He was solid back then, always the one we could count on. Ten years have changed everything, it appears.

Jori and Nicky stir in the back seat. They want out. As though they have evoked some memory in Steve, he reaches in to touch them. He is halfway into the car, but I hear him mumble something about a son of his own. "Can't even see the little guy."

I watch the glow at the end of his cigarette as it dangles precariously and am relieved when he finally pulls himself back out of the car window. I unbuckle the children from their seats, but I wish they were tucked in their beds for their afternoon naps.

I do not feel safe, even standing in our own front yard at 3:30 in the afternoon. Currents of fear begin to carry my mind through every bit of news I've ever heard about rape, murder, and drug-related crimes. Even if we did know Steve once, we don't know him now.

The children run through the grass in perfect normalcy while I try to think what to do. I have just suggested that Steve come back later when I see Mark's yellow Vega coming down the street. The crisis is passed, or so I suspect. Mark is the professional minister trained for emergency. He knows what to do with people who vary from the norm. He will take Steve out for coffee, sober him up, or whatever it takes to ensure he is not a nuisance to the public safety. I will be glad to see them go. Children do not need to be exposed to cracked utopia this early in their lives. Let them sleep the sleep of innocence while they can.

Several hours pass. I put the rhubarb on to cook and arrange the gladioluses into a centerpiece for the dinner table. When Mark returns, Steve is still with him. He sits on the front porch step while Mark comes into the kitchen to talk.

"The guy's desperate. I took a loaded .22-caliber pistol from him. He's planning to kill himself, says he can't live his hell any longer. The next twenty-four hours are critical, and I can't leave him alone. We need to keep him here, feed him dinner, and let him sleep on the couch in the family room. What do you say?"

I am standing in my kitchen on Dunton Street, talking to my husband, watching through the window as the children swing on swings, and stirring cornstarch mixture into roast beef drippings to make gravy. But I am not only on Dunton Street making gravy; I am also a child of six, sitting with my legs dangling from a crude wooden bench in an Alabama State Farm Penitentiary. . . .

The walls were as gray as the weather outside that day so long ago. My mother and daddy were there because they had been invited to conduct services. They brought their children because we were a family. Not many outsiders partook of activity behind the high electric wires that penned men in for life, but the guards knew us at a glance and the gates swung wide for our black 1949 Ford. We followed the sandy road that led to the barracks where the cafeteria was housed. The men would be waiting for us, seated in orderly rows on backless benches.

We had no fear as we walked between the rows of prisoners and the security guards in green who stood at attention along the side walls. I didn't feel the need to take my mother's hand. The men were our friends. Ashley, doing life for murder, was a small, neat man who always sat at the end of row three. He would shout out "Hymn number 51" when Daddy asked for favorite songs, and he was usually the first to his feet when the time came for testimonies. I'd never thought to be afraid of Ashley; all that really mattered was that he now loved God and gave away Juicy Fruit gum to my brother Jimmie and me after the service was over.

I was surrounded by one hundred gray uniforms— hardened criminals who were serving time for murder, rape, or theft. I swung my legs to the beat of the music. We sang, the prisoners and I, as though there were no differences between us. The Cross was the same. Time would teach me to fear, but I didn't learn it in that place, as dangerous as it could have been.

I always looked for Seisemore in the audience. He was big and burly and reminded me of a stuffed teddy bear. Seisemore smiled a lot, even across the scar that ran the width of his chin. It came, no doubt, from the days when he was outlawed in the dense woods of western Alabama. "Armed and dangerous" was the only way folks knew him in those days. Finally, the law had caught up with him. He hoed cabbage on the penitentiary truck farm during the day, and every first Sunday of the month he came to hear the preacher who often stopped to put his arm around the prisoners. Prisoners didn't get many hugs those days, and Seisemore seemed to need all the hugs he could get.

No wonder that on November 1, 1950, when the preacher preached from Isaiah 45:22—"Look to Me, and be saved"—Seisemore, the big, burly man who once played roulette with his life, cried like a baby and knelt at the altar bench in front of my dad. My mother played "Just as I Am, Without One Plea'" softly on the piano, and I cried right along with Seisemore. Even at age six, I recognized the miracle of redemption when I saw it. I watched my dad wipe tears from his eyes, too. Then he knelt on the floor beside Seisemore, put his arm around him, and guided him into the kingdom.

There was no fear in that place, only glory among the formerly armed and dangerous. And I was there to share the glory, not tucked safely away in bed among my teddy bears. I was there to swing my legs from the bench, sing "On a hill far away . . . ," chew Juicy Fruit gum, and see hardened criminals come to the Cross. I was there because Mother and Daddy wanted me to see the glory. It was a risk, the place was not all safe, but I saw redemption there among the rubble. . . .

But today, standing in my kitchen on Dunton Street, I do not see redemption. I see only the fallen world in which I live. I am not at home in this rubble because I was created for Eden, where humans are 100 percent trustworthy and there are no .22-caliber pistols to remind me of danger. By nature, I prefer gardens where I can pick rhubarb and gladioluses, where there are no men with tattooed arms and gold serpent chains waiting on my front porch. I would rather not have to look into glazed eyes and wonder whether my children are safe.

I fear the unpredictability of this fallen Eden where Satan has been given free rein for a while. I am suspicious of the evil that infests people and their minds. I watch the scenario of malice that unfolds every morning in the news or spreads itself across the TV screen. And after a while, I lose sight of trust. I am so preoccupied with protecting myself that I forget that man can be redeemed. Even more tragic, I may close myself off from the very people who need the glory the most.

But God's plan is redemption, not safety. If I would live in Eden, I would not see redemption, for it is not necessary in the Garden. There is no need to buy back what has never been sold, to restore what has never been damaged, or to free what has never been enslaved.

So God's world has sold itself down the river. It is sometimes armed and dangerous. It shows up unexpectedly wearing red headbands, gold serpents on a chain, and blue tattoos on its forearms. And no, it's not safe. But how else could it be redeemable? How would we ever see the glory if we were still in Eden? How will I witness redemption if I only pick rhubarb and arrange gladioluses in a vase?

I cannot live in Eden. Thousands of years ago, I was asked to leave. The cherubim and the flaming sword are still there, flashing back and forth to guard the way to the tree of life (see Gen. 3:24). I must walk among the rubble where redemption can flourish.

If I would learn risk, I must commit myself to a walk among danger when obedience calls for it. I will not live carelessly or without thought, but when fallenness comes to my door and sits on my porch steps, I must follow the higher call and trust God for my safety. I cannot both protect and see the glory of redemption.

If I would risk, I must return to the cause of my fear. I must sit with Moses on a log in the plains of Midian, on the far side of the desert, and receive the divine command to return to Pharaoh, the very person I fear the most. I must take that long, painful journey back to the place of my bondage and stand stuttering and stammering, rubbing my sweaty hands on my tunic, trying to swallow the panic that clogs my throat as I face Pharaoh, the one I fear. If I would know freedom and the Promised Land, I must start with Pharaoh.

If I would risk, I must analyze the fears that bind me. Where do they come from? Where are they taking me? Are they real or imagined? How are they affecting the people around me? What effect do they have on my obedience to God? Do I need professional help—Aaron, the expert— when I stand before my fears?

Sometimes, to be free to risk, I must simply call fear by its name. Describe it to a friend, to a spouse, to God, or to my journal. Sometimes I must visualize the process of giving it up. "Lord, this fear is not from You" (see 2 Tim. 1:7), so I wrap it up, tie it securely with string, and deposit it at the Cross where all burdens are meant to be brought. Once it is thus deposited, I must walk away and leave it there.

On the journey into risk, I must always consider redemption more important than safety. I must walk with Queen Esther of the Old Testament along gilded halls on my way to the throne room. Only those who have been summoned may stand before the king. But I must go, even without invitation, for the lives of my people are at stake. I must stand tall and firm against evil—Haman, right-hand man to the king, who has ordered the execution of my people. Will I ever walk the halls again? I don't know, but I walk in the conviction that "whoever loses his life for My sake . . . will save it" (Mark 8:35). I must lose my life, even as I head toward the throne room. If I perish, I perish. I must acknowledge possible consequences but enter the throne room anyhow. It is a walk for redemption's sake.

The man still waits on my front porch steps. Uncertainty pounds against the temples of my forehead, and I close my eyes to ease the pressure. Keep him overnight? But is he safe? What if he comes for his gun in the middle of the night? What if he tries to kill himself with my kitchen knives? What if he harms the children?

I stand before Pharaoh. I am afraid, but I remember the glory among the rubble. I remember big, burly Seisemore, murderer of men, kneeling by a crude wooden bench, crying tears of repentance. If my parents had played it safe, I would have missed the glory. I did not miss it then, and I will not miss it today.

I take a deep breath. "Yes," I answer Mark. "Let's keep him here." I set another place at the dinner table, put out the guest towels in the bathroom, and explain to the children that we will have company for the night.

Years have passed since that desperate man sat on our front porch steps. I didn't sleep that night, even though the only disruption was in my mind. But today I see the glory. His family lives with the scars, but they have been reunited and welcomed into the care of a body of believers. Sometimes when I find myself avoiding the rubble, pulling in the safety latch, I remember a gold serpent on a chain, and I find courage to risk the walk among danger.

5

Snowstorms and Stolen Watches

Control

The snow piles like giant fifteen-foot waves down the middle of Twenty-second Street, along Laramie Avenue, and into the church parking lot. The elevated train tracks are just a stone's throw to the left, but I haven't heard a train for several days. If you love adventure, it's your kind of day. Otherwise, you look for a good book and settle down by the light of a candle. Electricity has long since been knocked out by the howling northwester, which is being dubbed "Midwest's storm of the century."

Today I don't settle down with a good book. I don't really love this kind of adventure, but I must climb the frozen drifts, brace the northwester, and cross the Laramie Avenue bridge. Sara lives on the other side, and she is waiting for my visit. She will have the coffee ready and will serve me kolacky on a silver-plated tray. She may even have her front-room radiators turned on so we can sit on her green satin couch. Sara is a person I can't disappoint, even during the worst blizzard of the century. Besides, I reason, her house isn't far, and the walk will do me good. I wrap myself in down and wool and go out into the sound and fury.

I'm right. Sara is looking for me. "Thought you'd never come," she yells down from the landing when I push the button that buzzes her apartment. Sara is not very tall, but what she lacks in height she makes up for in the force of her personality. She peers over her wire-rimmed glasses as I mount the stairs. Her red hair is cropped short, almost mannish, and her jaw is square, firm and set. I always felt that if Sara ever got angry, I would want to stay far away.

But I know her gentle side, too. She helps me unwind my frozen scarf and hangs my wet coat on the clothes tree in the hall. The tree leans like the Tower of Pisa, but Sara doesn't appear to notice. Even if she did, she could do little about it. In fact, there isn't much Sara can do about anything. For her, life is a carousel of horses, galloping in place, going nowhere. Only her carousel has no lights or music, just three rooms in a row, two windows facing north, and a few scattered trinkets decorating the walls. Today her face looks more set than usual. Perhaps it's the weather.

The front-room radiator is on, and in the afternoon's gray I see the silver-plated tray of goodies waiting for me. Despite her stoic existence, she seems to draw meaning from serving me kolacky on silver, even if the silver is plated. She doesn't have to ask anymore what I take in my coffee; she goes ahead and puts in the cream and stirs it as though presiding over a ritual.

Sara finds meaning not only in ritual but also in tedious detail. She reviews her week for me. Cush, her Great Dane, has had his rabies shot; the factory where she works has laid off another eight people; the pipes under her sink still leak after three weeks, even though the landlord keeps promising to repair them. It's the story of her life. Broken promises and broken ties.

I have heard the story often, each time with variation. I come today and all the other days of my friendship with Sara to help her rewrite her script, to introduce her to hope, to see the hard edges of her face soften and, perhaps someday, to see her smile. I suspect she once knew how, but the years have taught her to forget. My hopes for Sara are bound up in my friendship to her and have been since that day two years ago, when we met in the Twenty-second Street Laundromat.

I'd forgotten detergent and had to borrow some. It wasn't a large need, but it drew us into conversation. I poured the soap, and Sara sat watching me as I told her where I'd come from and what I did. When she heard Mark and I were in church youth work, she went from casual lender of the soap to active participant in the story. She'd once had a teen. She told me about it, matter-of-factly and without emotion, like telling me the grass is green. She stared straight ahead as she talked, her eyes riveted on the change machine. Perhaps she didn't want anyone to see into her soul. I got the feeling she was used to protecting herself.

Her voice was low and husky. "My daughter walked out two years ago. Left a note but never told me where she was going, and I don't 'spect it would matter much if she had told me. She was almost seventeen." Sara paused as though trying to decide whether it was safe to go on with this stranger who couldn't remember to bring soap to the Laundromat. Apparently, it was.

"Her daddy left me before she was born. Haven't heard from him in twenty years, though I think he went back to Louisiana where his family is. Maybe Lisa went to find him. She often talked about it. Anyhow, now it's just me and the dog . . ." Then almost as an afterthought, she added, "I've learned not to count on anyone. All they'll do is let you down."

That was her commentary on life. Never expect anything, then you're never disappointed. I wondered what gave her any reason to get up in the morning. Certainly, she didn't live to sit in the Laundromat and watch the clothes go around. Did she know anything about hope? We were just one washer cycle into conversation, and already I felt myself being drawn in.

Sara fast became my friend, and consequently, my mission. I often dropped by the yellow brick apartment building where she lived to see how she was doing. At first we stood in the hall and talked about life at the tool and die company where she worked. She never invited me in—her way of not counting on me, I supposed. Finally, one evening she asked if I would like a cup of coffee. I sat in her kitchen with my coat on all evening and drank black Sanka. That was the night she pointed to the crucifix hanging above her sink.

"It doesn't mean anything to me, but I leave it there for my mother—may God rest her soul in peace," she said almost apologetically, like someone who had promised something and then not delivered. Sara never got around to offering me another cup of coffee that night, but she did seem thoughtful after I told her that the cross was very meaningful to me because it showed me how much I was loved by God.

Then one evening, months later, Sara invited Mark and me to dinner. That night she took our coats and even turned on the heat registers in her front room. Mark and I talked freely about our lives, our faith, and our work at the church.

"Someday I'm going to come to your church. Seems like I might could use it, although I sure hope they don't ask for money," she said.

When it was time for us to leave, she went into her bedroom and came out with a china teapot. Without looking at me, as though to avoid feeling, she put it into my hand. Giving was awkward for her. I could tell.

"Why don't you take this home with you. I don't drink tea anyway. It came from Scotland. My great-grandfather gave it to my mother. He was Scottish, you know." Then, as though she didn't want to count on anything too much, she hurried us into our coats and out the door. I saw the light in the front room go out before we'd even reached the corner.

Today, a year and a half later, as I sit in Sara's front room and watch the storm outside, I wonder how much longer it will be until hope comes to her. She knows about religion, but religion without God depresses. Only religion with God brings hope. And Sara shows few signs of need for either. I'm sure time and love will win. I'm satisfied to know I'm doing all I can for Sara. She listens, respects, talks, and loves to have me visit. Hope will follow.

"Ruth, do you ever have physical checkups?" Sara's question comes out of the blue as I bite into a piece of kolacky. She doesn't even wait for my answer; she apparently is looking for an opportunity to tell me about herself. I hear a new edge to her voice. Another layer of protection, no doubt.

"I haven't been to a doctor in eighteen years. Never had time for them. All they want is your money. I figure, when your time is up, your time is up, doctor or not. I've had a lump in my breast for some time. Now it's getting bigger. Believe I might stop by the clinic down there on Thirty-first Street. I've heard they have sliding scale payments. Lots of people probably live with lumps in their breasts . . ."

She stops as though she's run out of words, or maybe she is about to run out of control. I struggle, too, only my struggle is for something to say, something to do.

I manage a few lines of assurances and comfort, but even as I talk, I feel helpless. Sara abruptly stands and hurries me toward the Leaning Tower of Pisa coat rack. She apparently isn't interested in comfort, but attempts lightheartedness.

"Anyhow now, you bundle up good when you walk back over that bridge. Can't have you freezing to death 'cause you came to see me. Mark would never forgive me. Here, take this tray with you. You'll use it more than I do. Take the kolacky, too. Mark might like some. Make him a cup of coffee and warm him up."

I am almost bent double against the wind as I push my way back across the Laramie Avenue bridge. I think about Sara all the way home.

When I call her apartment the next Friday, there is no answer. I try late into the night but without success. Finally, in desperation, I follow my hunches and call the hospital. Sara was admitted two days ago, the same day as her checkup.

Two days in the hospital and she hasn't even bothered to call. I consider myself her friend, one of the few faithful ones she has, according to her. What does it mean when you go to the hospital without telling your friend? You don't want to be bothered? You are afraid to have anyone care? You can't bring yourself to admit there's anything wrong? You're running from hope? I don't know how to interpret her silence.

I also don't know how to interpret my sense of loss. Sara is still alive; she is still my friend, even though she hasn't been very good at keeping me informed. I suspect I am grieving for more than Sara.

Perhaps it's loss of momentum—something to do for Sara. Visiting her apartment, drinking coffee, taking her dog for a walk, going with her to the Laundromat. Perhaps I am grieving God's apparent silence. I have prayed consistently, long and hard for Sara—as I walked to her apartment, drove down her street, passed her factory; as I washed clothes at the Laundromat; after I had a conversation with her on the phone. Anytime I thought of Sara, I prayed, "Salvation, please." But I have no indication my prayers have made any difference. Nothing significant about Sara has changed.

I call the hospital, talk to Sara, and then pull out her silver-plated tray and serve chocolate chip cookies and hot tea from it. It's a bleak reminder. Sara doesn't even want me to come to the hospital. She told me so over the phone, but I vow to go anyway. I must know what is happening to her. I tuck my New Testament into my purse as I go out the door.

I find myself rushing to get to the elevated train platform to wait. The ride to the hospital isn't long, but I feel as though I have a long way to go. In many ways, I do. A

65

giant clock ticks in my head, and it's winding down.

The pink roses I've brought look somehow out of place in the lifelessness of the cancer ward. Sara's eyes are closed when I walk in. Her bobbed hair is a mat of red against her head, and her face and sheets are about equal in their whiteness. Sara seems to sense my presence. She squints to see me, then reaches out her hand to greet me. "So much pain, Ruth. So much pain. You can't imagine . . ."

I'm taken aback by the change—so much in such a short time—as though the cancer has finally called its trump. I pull up a chair and sit beside her bed. She mumbles on, tired and weak, a jumble of trivia—almost like the life she lives. I hear about the institutional food, the snoring neighbors on her wing who keep her from sleeping, the sponge baths, the nurses' station, the doctors, the lab technicians, her roommate who went home yesterday— endless trivia, as though talking is the only reassurance she has. Maybe if she talks long enough, this ugly nightmare will go away. Maybe the clinic got it all wrong: there really is no lump in her breast, and there's no need for tomorrow's surgery. Maybe if we talk trivialities, we won't get around to need.

But I get around to need anyway, even though I don't call it by name. I ask Sara if I may read to her from the Bible. I choose the Twenty-third Psalm, which is indexed in the back of my New Testament, "For those in need of comfort." Sara has not admitted to need, but I assume the comfort part applies to her. She closes her eyes while I read:

> The LORD is my shepherd;
> I shall not want. . . .
> He leads me beside the still waters. . . .
> He leads me in the paths of righteousness. . . .

Surely goodness and mercy shall follow me
All the days of my life;
And I will dwell in the house of the LORD
Forever.

"Reminds me of my mother," she says with her eyes still closed. "You are a good girl to come all this way to see me. Really isn't worth your time. Just get me through this surgery tomorrow, and I'll make it. They can't keep an old bag like me down."

I can tell she is tired, and visiting hours are soon over. I hug her good-bye and take one look back as I go through the door. Her eyes are closed again, and her face is set in its familiar firmness. She is facing her illness as she has faced the rest of her life—stoic, hard, wrapped in her shell of protection. Perhaps she feels it would hurt too much the other way.

For Sara, it's the beginning of the end. Over the next six months she walks in the shadow. At times I feel the shadow with her, dark and menacing, stalking on all fours to gobble up both of us. She admits to pain, but never to need. I try, but I cannot make it happen. The weaker she grows, the harder I try. I continue to pray privately. I pray with Sara. I read verses of comfort, hope, and conviction. I bring her roses, books, and a radio for quiet hymns of faith to ease her through her sleepless nights.

The snow piles turn to slush, and the promise of spring renews my efforts. Life is born from death. There is still hope tangled in with all the painkillers, tubes, wires, and monitors of the heart. But Sara's condition worsens, and the clock winds down. Finally, I don't even feel like going to the hospital anymore. I force myself, but I see no response to hope and little response to life.

Tonight, it's over. Her chance for hope and my plans to see change in her have scattered like loose pages on a windy day. As far as I know, she wore her shell of protection to the grave. I cry for my loss. For her loss. I feel the dark night. I am standing on shore watching an empty boat as it drifts aimlessly across the bar; the waves mock it . . . no hope . . . no hope . . . no hope. I did it all for Sara, but it was not enough. Except for a last-minute miracle of grace, she chose to die without making a verbal commitment to Christ as her Savior. And if there was a miracle, I will never know, this side of heaven.

The voice at the other end of the line is flat and unmoving—with a tone similar to Sara's. He is the brother she hasn't seen for ten years. "There won't be much of a funeral. We will have a priest. But Sara did ask that you bring a eulogy. It was her one request."

A eulogy? Praise for what? Coffee and snowstorms and kolacky on a silver-plated tray? Commendation for what? For watching clothes go around in a Laundromat? I have given enough. Why give more when I will never know the results? I'm tired. Disappointed. Grieving loss. Why set myself up for standing in front of people at the funeral and losing control completely? I have lost enough already. . . .

At one time control didn't matter, and mission was for the pure joy of service, not for the results or trophies to be collected at the end. It was there in Alabama where the sand was warm beneath my bare feet and the pines fragrant above my head, there in Alabama where by eight o'clock in the morning I could already feel the sultry breezes blowing in from the gulf, sixty miles away. That time of the year, the breezes clung to the body like steamy comforters.

I was still in bed when I recognized the sound of Mary Francis's old blue pickup truck as it rattled its way across the iron bars of the cattlegap—iron bars laid parallel into the ground that served to keep wandering cows out of the yard and also to announce unexpected guests. Actually, most of our guests were unexpected, so the cattlegap came in quite handy.

I quickly pulled on my sundress and ran out to welcome the truckload of Mary Francis and her four brothers who were yelping like dogs and jumping around the back of the truck like they'd just been unleashed.

I wasn't sure why they'd come to the house. Maybe they came to borrow gas. Maybe to report on how Eila Mae was doing with her bout of flu. Maybe they'd come for breakfast. Maybe they showed up for no reason at all. With Mary Francis, there didn't have to be a reason.

Mary Francis came in and plopped herself down at the kitchen table. It was obvious she intended to stay, but that wasn't a problem. We were going to wash clothes and freeze corn. My mother would have extra help.

"Hello, Mary Francis," Mother greeted her. "You're up bright and early. How is everyone at your house? Would you like some muffins? Take some out to your brothers, too."

My mother headed toward the garage with a basket of dirty clothes. She looked crisp and cool in her white cotton dress with little blue flowers. Her black wavy hair was drawn up in a knot at the nape of her neck. No matter how hot the day or how much work we had to do or how many unexpected guests, Mother always seemed cool. Perhaps that was why people liked to be around her.

Mary Francis and I helped ourselves to the muffins and took what was left to the boys who were climbing the ropes of the swing. Apparently, they never thought of sitting on the board seat and swinging. The muffins brought them down from the heights in a hurry. My brothers, Jimmie and Denny, finished their breakfast out by the swing, and the day was off to a favorable start.

It seemed as if Mary Francis had always been around—from the first Sunday of church services in our garage to now, almost nine months later. She had sat attentively on the front row that first Sunday, cracked her gum, and twirled a lock of her long black hair, never taking her eyes off my daddy as he preached. She had been the first to shake the preacher's hand afterward and the first to tell him that next time she'd bring her whole family. Besides, she'd like to win the Bible for inviting the most people to Sunday school.

Mary Francis had won the Bible, and she told us she would read it every day. Finally, she had decided that the message of redemption was for her. Then, on a Sunday afternoon, some months later, we had stood by Sampson Creek and sung, "Oh happy day that fixed my choice on thee my Savior and my God," as Mary Francis was baptized.

But Mary Francis didn't show up just for church services. She came for everything in between as well. No one seemed to mind. Whatever was happening at the time continued, and Mary Francis joined right in. If we were eating, she ate. Working, she worked. If we were sitting on the front porch, she sat on the front porch, cracked her gum, and watched the sunset with us. Mother always treated her like an honored guest, often talking to her about the Bible and the greatness of God. I knew Mother and Daddy were pleased with the progress Mary Francis was making in her faith.

Now Mary Francis and I stepped over the piles of clothes lining the garage floor. Mary Francis laughed. "This here pile of underwear is where the preacher stands to preach."

Mother was already guiding pieces of clothing through the two rotating cylinders of the wringer washing machine and into the round tin tub of rinse water. The wagonload of freshly pulled corn waited outside under a shade tree beside the picnic table. I couldn't remember seeing a higher mountain of corn.

"You and Mary Francis can go ahead and get started on the corn," Mother said from across the washtub. "Be sure you get all the silk off the ears, and here, take these gunny sacks to put the husks in."

Mary Francis and I made ourselves as comfortable as possible on the picnic table benches and started working on the corn. I was sorry we had had such a plentiful year, but it did help that Mary Francis was there, even if she did crack her gum and smell of sweat even before there was anything to sweat about. We started by singing every gospel chorus we could think of. Gospel choruses and songs were new to Mary Francis, but she knew almost as many as I did and hardly ever missed a word. Mother and Daddy joined the cornhusking party, and Daddy even pulled the boys in from out of the trees to help.

We husked. We pulled off silk. We boiled the ears in big pots on the stove, then cut the blanched corn from the cob. As we cut with the knives Daddy had sharpened, kernels of cut corn flew everywhere, landing in our hair, on our noses, in our laps, and all over the newspaper Mother had wisely spread on the picnic table.

Six hours and sixty quarts of corn later, we washed the last cooking pot, folded up the messy newspapers, and took the corn husks out to the pig. Our clean clothes had long since been folded and put back in the drawers and closets. The boys propped themselves up by the side of the garage and drew pictures in the dirt with a stick. All of us began to wind down, but I could tell Mother was pleased with our day's accomplishments. She thanked Mary Francis and company for their help and gave them all a big hug.

"Shore did enjoy my day, Miz Hollinger. Hope your corn tastes good."

Mother gave her several quarts of the finished product to take home, and Mary Francis and her brothers waved good-bye as they rattled back across the cattlegap and disappeared in a fog of dust.

We were just sitting down to dinner when Mother discovered her watch was missing from the window ledge above the washing machine where she had laid it when she started the laundry.

"Are you sure this is where you put it?" Daddy asked as he pulled the washing machine out from the wall.

Mother was sure, but just in case she checked the little white ivory box with the velvet lining that sat on her bedroom dresser. The watch was not there. The watch never left Mother's arm except when she put it in the velvet box or on the window ledge above the washing machine. The meatballs and mashed potatoes got cold on the table while we scoured the house, looking for the missing watch. In the garage, under the knotty pine wall cabinets Daddy had built. In the house, under beds, rugs, chairs, Daddy's desk in the living room. Out in the yard, around the picnic table, under the swing, even out as far as the gas pump and the barn. We looked everywhere, but there was not a trace of Mother's gold watch.

We were a sober lot as we finally sat down to our cold dinner. The watch that had disappeared from the shelf in the garage was not just an ordinary watch. It was the one reminder my mother had of Aunt May. My mother had been only four years old when her mother died, and Aunt May had become the one person who could fill the empty spaces in the heart of a little girl without a mother. Aunt May had been the mother my mother had never known. And when the time came for Mother to leave Pennsylvania to do pioneer church work in southern Alabama with her young husband, Aunt May was like a piece of Mother's heart left behind.

I remembered the morning almost a year ago when someone had driven ten miles out from town to bring Mother the message that Aunt May had died. She simply went to sleep and never woke up. Aunt May was only thirty-eight.

I remembered standing there in the middle of the living room floor and watching my mother cry. Daddy held her close, but other than that, no one seemed to know exactly what to do. I sat on the couch and cried for my mother, not for Aunt May whom I barely knew. Jimmie stood beside Mother and patted her arm while Denny went to find some Kleenex. It was not every day we saw our mother cry.

Several months later an odd-shaped package had arrived in the mail, containing a piece of paper with Uncle John's neat printing. *"Dear Gertie. This watch was my gift to your Aunt May on our wedding day. You were as dear to her as her own boys. I hope you will wear the watch and remember how much your aunt loved you. I love you, too. Uncle John."*

The watch was beautiful, small and dainty with a tiny

red ruby in the center. I loved to touch it and look at it when it was on my mother's arm. It had been a reminder to me of how God had cared for a four-year-old motherless girl. Now that the watch was gone, all my mother had left of Aunt May were memories, and one cannot touch memories.

We ate our meal in silence. No one said it, but we all thought: *Mary Francis was the only person outside our family who had been in the garage today. Her brothers had never even come inside.*

Finally, as I was getting ready for bed, I blurted out to my mother, "Mary Francis always did like that watch. I saw her looking at it today. She stole it. I know it. I know it. She is mean and ugly, and I don't ever want to see her again."

I cried in anger for my mother's loss. I was only seven, but I knew what being taken advantage of meant. After all my mother and father had done for Mary Francis and her family. I remembered the day my mother had taken one of her own sweaters and given it to Mary Francis so she wouldn't have to go to school cold, not to mention all the times Mary Francis and her family had mooched food off our table. I didn't care if she did help us put up sixty quarts of sweet corn today or could sing all the gospel choruses and had been baptized in Sampson Creek. She was a thief.

"Now, Ruth Ann. We don't know Mary Francis took the watch. It's a serious thing to accuse people of stealing."

Mother thanked me for my concern, then knelt by my bed and prayed that we would know how to respond to the missing watch. Her voice was low and sorrowful. I knew how much she loved that watch. I also knew how much she loved Mary Francis and her family. It was a sad night for my mother, and I would not forgive Mary Francis for the hurt she had caused.

Sunday came, and still there was no watch. Mother casually asked Mary Francis if she had seen the gold watch lying on the window sill when she was over the other day.

Mary Francis blew a giant bubble with her bubble gum and in a jumpy voice said, "No ma'am. I ain't seen no watch."

I did notice how quickly she walked away from my mother after that. Anytime she caught me looking at her, she looked the other way. Mary Francis was not herself that day. I was more sure than ever that she had taken Aunt May's watch.

When it was time for the church service to begin, Mary Francis marched to the front row and flopped down on the wooden folding chair right in front of Daddy's pulpit. I hoped Daddy would preach on the Ten Commandments. Mary Francis could use a good dose of "Thou shalt not steal." Instead Daddy chose his text from John 15:13: "Greater love has no one than this, than to lay down one's life for his friends."

Daddy's gray eyes always shone when he preached, and his wide smile showed his perfectly white teeth. I thought I could listen to him forever. That morning he seemed to preach with even more gentleness, though I wished for Mary Francis's sake he had been a little more gruff.

Sunday dinner was often a community affair. Mother usually invited the church folk to stay and eat—Mary Francis and her family usually stayed. I secretly hoped Mother would skip Mary Francis and her family, but right after the benediction, as Mother went around and hugged all the women and children, I heard her say to Mary Francis's mother, "Y'all stay and have some dinner with us. I've put on some of the corn Mary Francis helped us do. There's plenty of food."

Of course, Mary Francis and her family accepted. Daddy and some of the men set up sawhorses and boards under the trees while Mother and I went for the white linen tablecloths and good dishes. Some folks had brought contributions to the dinner table—butter beans, black-eyed peas, turnip greens, fried chicken, and pecan pie. I noticed that Mary Francis and her family hadn't brought anything. Daddy carried out three one-gallon jugs of iced tea and set them on the end of the table, then he called everyone together and thanked God for the love that surrounded the table of food. I was irritated that he kept talking about love.

I couldn't help glaring across the table at Mary Francis as she dug into a heaping pile of chicken and dumplings that my mother had made. She didn't deserve to sit at our table and eat our food. She was a fake for singing the gospel songs and stealing at the same time. I wondered what she had done with the watch. I was certain we would never see it again.

And we didn't, to this very day. But after a while, I stopped thinking about the watch and about Mary Francis, the thief. Every now and then I stopped by the white ivory box that sat empty on Mother's dresser. I looked at the box and got a sad feeling in my throat and my eyes. But Mother and Daddy never changed in their actions toward Mary Francis. She kept right on dropping by at any hour of the day or night. Mother continued to feed her, listen to her, and talk to her about the greatness of God. Mary Francis continued to come to every service, sit on the front row, memorize the Scripture verses, and sing the gospel songs without missing a word. And Mother and

Daddy continued to treat her just as though she was an honored guest.

———————— 🐦 ————————

But I do not so easily continue when I've been disappointed. Once let down, my inclination is to either close out the efforts completely or double my attempts to change the circumstances, reform the person, pray, or talk another into submission. My instinct is to control and to slip it in under the guise of parenting, prayer, God's will, or my personality.

When I must be in control, I have reduced God to formula. I have, as it were, captured Him in a bottle and slapped on a label: this is how He must work in order for Him to be God. When I must control, I have reduced the personhood of others to no more than that of a robot by cutting off their option to choose. If disobedience is not an option, neither is love. When I must control, I have reduced myself, focusing on the result rather than the process, on outcome rather than obedience. If I must always be in control, I write myself off as a failure when my plans go astray.

But God's call to me is not a call to control. It is a call to risk giving Him the options. His thoughts are not my thoughts, His ways, not my ways. He is the wind, a current of air that drifts in and out of unexpected places, working in ways I had not planned. Who am I to try to catch Him in a glass jar and control His movements? Who am I to retreat in failure because I cannot see the wind?

If I would learn to risk, I must be willing to let the loose ends fly sometimes. I must mentally give up my need for life to be nailed down in perfect order. Sometimes the formulas don't work. Sometimes a friend dies without preparing herself for eternity, even when you have been a faithful witness. Sometimes a trusted convert steals your watch, even when you have poured out your soul in service to her. I must be content to know that God is at work in His world, even when I do not see how He is at work.

I must be willing to dare out-of-controlness for a while. I will not be lazy, careless, or noncommittal, but if I would risk, I must let the Spirit of God carry the details of my life where He will, whether or not it means a spotless house, immaculate children, or a completed list of accomplishments for the day.

If I would risk, I must be willing to live with unfulfilled dreams. I must climb the rocky slopes of Mount Nebo, just east of the Promised Land. With Moses, I must stand and gaze into the fertile green of the Jordan Valley, knowing I will never walk that valley. I will never be honored at a retirement dinner, never be awarded a gold watch or a walnut plaque to hang on my office wall for my years of faithful service and dedication.

Oh, but I deserve the praise! I have endured endless years of complaining, grumbling people who took from me more than I could ever give. I have felt their hunger pains with them, burned my feet on the hot desert floor, worked from sunup to sundown settling their differences for them, reading the law to them, and seeking the face of God for them. But I am left with nothing to show for it except a lonely mountaintop where jagged rocks jut into the air, the wind blows cold, and old men come to die.

With Moses, I must offer praise even when I am no longer in control. I must bless Joshua, the new leader. In my disappointment, I must call my people together before I return one last time to the mountaintop. I must raise my voice against the open air, across the valley where the people gather en masse, and offer my tribute of thanksgiving:

> *Remember the days of old,*
> *Consider the years of many generations. . . .*
> *He found him in a desert land*
> *And in the wasteland, a howling wilderness;*
> *He encircled him, He instructed him,*
> *He kept him as the apple of His eye. . . .*
> *So the* LORD *alone led him (Deut. 32:7–12).*

If I would truly know risk, I must thank God even when I am not in control. I must accept people as they are rather than try to manipulate them to be what I think they should be. I must let the wind blow free, learning to enjoy, rather than resist, the unpredictables. I must offer my service without focus on reward. I must eulogize even when I feel I have nothing to say.

I stand by Sara's coffin, before a tiny group of mourners: some family members, a few friends from the tool and die works, and Sara's priest. The funeral home is dark and musty. I take a deep breath and try to steady the yellow tablet paper in front of me. The room is blurry, the paper smudged. But I give praise.

I praise snowstorms and kolacky, teapots from Scotland and silver-plated trays. I praise walks over the Laramie Avenue bridge and the gift of detergent in a Laundromat on Twenty-second Street. The priest clears his throat, and the silent brother of ten years lets the tears flow down his cheeks unashamedly. Afterward he comes to me, and with quivering voice he says, "You showed me a Sara I have never seen." For a moment I see softness in his hard exterior. His hand is shaking as he reaches out and squeezes mine. "I needed to know that about her. Thank you."

And today, years removed from my final farewell to Sara, when I struggle to control God's work in another's life, I remember a musty funeral home and Sara's brother with tears in his eyes. From that memory, I somehow draw courage to risk giving God the option to work in ways I have never planned—perhaps even to soften Sara's brother's heart, when I'd intended the softness for her.

PART TWO

RISK TAKING

Where Do I Begin?

6

Of Course I'm Scared, But ...

Willingness to Obey When You Don't Feel Like It

All the world is angry, or so it seems, as I stand here in the doorway of classroom N14 and look at the scowling man I assume to be the professor. I have signed up for Oral Interpretation of English Literature with high hopes for some academic relief from the restless mood of the university campus in this summer of the late 1960s. For those of us who have come to the university for educational purposes, the activities of the antiwar, antigovernment, antiblack, and antiestablishment crowd have been unwelcome intruders. Up until this point, I haven't noticed the mood infiltrating the classroom. Today, as I look at the man up front, I sense that the mood of the professor fits the mood of the times.

There is, it seems, no way of escaping this national sore

that festers on this urban campus. As I take my seat on the third row of the concrete pie-shaped classroom, I feel as though I am looking at yet another scene from the continuing saga of rage.

Six months ago, the rage had spread to the near West Side where it burned whole sections of Madison Street. We had stood in our third-floor apartment and looked due east toward the city where billows of black smoke rose like a giant inkblot against the sky.

The anger had come as far as our neighborhood, where three thousand helmeted National Guardsmen stood row upon row with bayonets and rifles poised at attention so that victims of injustice could march for their rights. We had been aliens in a strange land then, having to pass checkpoints for identification clearance as we came and went from our own homes.

For the last year and a half, anger has hung over the university as well. We have seen it daily in the open-air forum on campus where the dissenters gather to vent their hostilities. We heard it one day in shouts and sirens and rocks crashing through the glass of the cafeteria where we'd gone to have our lunch. We had looked down on a mass of hysteria—bottles and pop cans flying, fists pounding the air. The angry surge of students pushed and shoved and screamed their insults at Chicago's police force who stood like a great blue wall with their billy clubs in rigid attention in front of them and gas masks hiding their faces. Bull horns blared orders for restraint, and in the background, sirens wailed and blue lights flashed. Blue-and-white paddy wagons moved onto the sidewalks, gathering up the violence like one gathers dirt from the floor. In the end, anger was restrained, but the ugly mood prevailed.

I decide today, as I take out my pen and prepare for the lecture, that the man's mood has nothing to do with me. He is not scowling at me in particular but probably at life in general. Other students enter the room as if they are walking into a morgue. No one says a word. Professor Blairston seems to have cast his spell over the entire room. He glares at the class over his wire-rimmed glasses and blows smoke into the air. The three large wrinkles in the middle of his forehead do not go away even when he starts reading the student roster. He seems to be spitting out the names as he goes along.

"Ms. Senter. Goals and purposes for this class."

I am the second name he has called on for response. I wonder why he's picked me since my name is near the end of the alphabet, but I mutter something about combining my love for literature and speech. He is in a hurry to move on before my sentence is completed. Obviously, he doesn't really want to know why I've taken the course. Perhaps it's his way of showing who is in charge. I am quite certain no one is in doubt. I feel his abrasiveness—like sandpaper over tender skin.

I am relieved when we move on to the syllabus. Perhaps the mechanics of the course will warm things up. Or at least maybe the man will stop scowling when he gets to great literature. But his scowl continues all the way through the syllabus and on into his interpretation of T. S. Eliot's "The Hollow Men."

> We are the hollow men
> We are the stuffed men. . . .
> Shape without form, shade without colour,
> Paralysed force, gesture without motion. . . .

No one moves. We are walking with Blairston in the

"dead land . . . cactus land . . . this valley of dying stars . . . this broken jaw of our lost kingdoms . . ." We are into nothingness where man has nothing significant to say, nothing significant to contribute, and where the world ends, "Not with a bang but a whimper."

He finishes the piece, and we sit in silence. One dare hardly breathe. I am not sure whether it's the effect of the piece or the effect of the man.

"Class dismissed." He says it gruffly as though he will be glad to see us go. We quietly close our notebooks and leave the concrete wedge. It's 12:55. I walk back through the catacombs of concrete that make up the lecture center, but I feel I have been to the cactus land. "The eyes are not here / There are no eyes here / In this valley of dying stars." I have met the hollow man, heard the whimper. It will take a great deal of courage to face him every day. I feel I am still standing at the cafeteria window and looking down on the turmoil. Only this time it's not fists pounding the air but a man scowling into the faces of his students.

For the next few weeks I try to forget the man's anger. Instead I wait patiently for another dramatic encounter with great literature. After all, it's the reason I took the class. But we are hopelessly snagged on Anglo-Saxon prosody—pyrrhics, trochees, spondees, and anapests. I feel we are learning a foreign language, and I did not take the course to learn archaic symbols and codes. My frustration builds as we move through the explicative mode of interpretation and on into the linguistic. I do not care about function, form, and mechanics. No one else in the class seems to either. We sit politely and tolerate the hour and wonder why he ever became a teacher. We sense students are his one obstacle to teaching. If it weren't for us, he might actually enjoy the classroom.

It soon becomes obvious that Blairston is not in teaching to learn from or engage in dialogue with his students either. One day in the midst of his theory of oral interpretation I raise my hand, not to interrupt, but to ask an honest question. "Do you think it might be possible that the interpretation of literature is as much mood and feeling as technique, perhaps that it cannot be learned but has to be felt?"

Blairston glares at me with his cold, steel blue eyes. He shows no signs of having heard the question. "Well, Ms. Senter. Perhaps you want to teach the course?"

A painful moment of silence follows, then some slight snickering around the room. It's not the first time he has leveled a student, and I suspect the snickering is a symptom of fear. Who knows if they will be next? I feel my face flush. I want to run for cover, but I pick up my pen and furiously scribble on my notebook page.

I make a mental note not to question him again. I will listen to his theories, put up with the agonizing technicalities, and perform my three lecture recitals according to his style, writing out beforehand every tone, gesture, and voice level. I will do it to get out from under his anger, pass the course, and move on to happier academics.

My first lecture recital is scheduled for tomorrow. I have spent weeks chopping up Gray's "Elegy Written in a Country Church-yard," dissecting it into sensory parts— auditory, visual, kinesthetic, thermal, olfactory, and tactile. My brain swims in stifling detail. My eyes are blurry as I stare at the twenty pages of typed critical analysis before me. I have rehearsed my presentation until I feel I have lost forever my ability or desire to interpret literature orally. I am stiff, nervous, uptight, and tired. I wonder if I were not better at oral interpretation before I took the class.

But zero hour arrives. I am physically shaking as I take my place behind the podium. I wish I had gotten a few more hours of sleep last night or at least not had coffee just before class. I take a deep breath, but I feel wooden as I stare down at the notations on my script: drop intonation, pick up tempo, lengthen syllables, lower vocal pitch.

It's not the way I read great literature, but it's the way I am reading great literature today. I agonize over every gesture. My mouth is so dry my tongue clicks with each word. I am not in Buckinghamshire, England, with Gray, strolling the peaceful evening countryside. I am standing at the point, reading a paper entangled in hopeless technicalities, and floundering miserably in self-conscious form.

"Ms. Senter, *what* are you doing?" Blairston interrupts me before I've finished page two. "I don't know when I've heard anything so awful."

I am stunned. This is a college course, and I am being demolished in front of the whole class. My friends in the audience stir nervously. I sense sympathy from them. But all I get are cold stares from Blairston, as though I am deliberately trying to discredit him and his theories by my performance.

I stand helplessly behind the podium, unsure what he wants me to do. I don't trust myself to attempt an answer or to go on. I only want to get out of here, to escape his awful scowl. I have stood enough of his harsh insensitivities. Then, as though he is acquainted with mercy killings, he says simply, "You may sit down."

My paper is a blur in front of me. The whole room is a

blur. I feel my stomach vibrating. I am on the verge of losing my composure, but the thought of tears and further humiliation restrains me. The minute the bell rings, I am out the door, not even bothering to ask what I should do next. I can't stand to look at him. I don't ever want to see him again. I will just disappear among the catacombs and never return. Forget advanced oral interpretation of English literature. I will settle on an incomplete, so I can keep my self-respect.

I can't even think logically as I walk to the train. All I know is what I feel—anger, hurt, humiliation, and rejection. By the time I unlock the door to our third-floor apartment, the flood gates are opened. "I will never go back to that class again," I say determinedly to Mark who has been sitting patiently listening to my hurt pouring out. I have never been more certain about anything in my life. . . .

But there was another time and place when I didn't want to go back. I didn't like the woods at night, but we had to go through them to the Drowns community where we were conducting two weeks of vacation Bible school. The woods were dense and came right up to the narrow road. Every now and then a branch reached out and scraped along the truck, almost like the night had arms and was trying to grab us. My brothers and I had learned to keep our arms inside. The night that waited for us at the edge of the road had 100,000 eyes: leaves, trunks, twigs, needles, ferns, flowers, weeds, and furry creatures, cloaked in scary shapes, watching us pass.

What mysteries were in those woods? We didn't know

for sure. Some had said moonshine stills and a band of moonshiners who came into the gas station-grocery store at Brady's Junction for provisions now and then but otherwise were illusive.

During the day, the big yellow school bus stopped at the one house that sat in the middle of the woods between Brady's Junction and the Drowns community. Lily Mae was nice and very normal, but whispers were that her daddy was one of the moonshiners. We saw him sitting on the front porch once when the bus stopped to pick up Lily Mae. We pressed our faces against the windows and looked at him like we were staring at some ancient fossil in a museum. None of us knew what a real live moonshiner looked like, and we didn't want to miss the chance of finding out.

Then there were the Ashley brothers. Their mother came to our Bible studies and vacation Bible school under the tent, but her boys roamed the woods, sat by the side of the road, or sometimes slept off their inebriation on the bench in front of the gas station.

Rumor had it that they made their money from moonshine, too, but they didn't hide out in the woods. We saw them now and then along the road or at the gas station. Someone told Daddy the Ashley brothers had said, "We don't want no church here, and if that there preacher gets too pushy, we'll show him his place."

We had been coming through the woods for nearly two years, and so far the Ashley brothers were all talk. Sometimes if they were at the gas station when we stopped, Daddy went up and talked to them. I usually looked the other way, they were so frightening, so big and unkempt. Their faces were dark with unshaved stubble, and their hair blew wildly in all directions. They usually wore big work boots and bib overalls. I didn't like the thought of what they could do to my daddy, especially if they were drunk.

Their mother, on the other hand, was a pleasant-looking grandmotherly type with silver hair pulled straight back and held in place with a rubber band. Her face bore deep wrinkles, and her hands were gnarled. She always had something nice to say about the dress I was wearing or the way Mother had braided my hair. It was hard to understand how such a nice lady could have four sons who could make so much trouble.

"Y'all come on over to dinner one night," Mrs. Ashley had said after Bible study at her neighbor's house one evening. The only thing I could think of was her boys, so I was hoping we would be busy that night and could not go. But I heard Mother say, "That sure is sweet of you, Mrs. Ashley. I'm sure we could come. Besides, my family loves your cornbread." I knew the matter was settled. We would eat with Mrs. Ashley, and I would pray that her boys had gone to Mobile to work in the shipyards as they sometimes did.

As it turned out, the boys never came home while we were there, and Mrs. Ashley's cornbread was as good as ever. I crumbled it up and mashed it in with my black-eyed peas. I didn't remember when I'd had a tastier meal, but I did keep my eye on the back door, just in case the boys came home.

Summer came and with it, Vacation Bible School in the Drowns community. We hadn't seen Mrs. Ashley's boys for some time. We hadn't even heard many rumblings about them lately. Maybe they decided it was okay for the preacher to conduct services in their community. But as we drove through the woods to Bible school, they suddenly emerged from among the 100,000 eyes of the night and staggered into the middle of the road, right in front of our truck, eyes glistening like creatures of the wild. I noticed brown bottles sticking out of their pockets. Above the truck motor, I heard their crude, harsh laughs, like thunder rumbling in the distance, only much more ominous.

Daddy swerved to miss them, but there was nowhere to go except into the woods. He put on the brakes, the dust flew, and we came to a sideways halt across the road. Once the dust settled, I saw the rifle, big, black, and bold, aimed directly into the windshield at Daddy.

I couldn't stand to look. I put my head into my brother Jimmie's lap. He was older than I by eighteen months and much stronger. He was the closest thing to safety. I closed my eyes and stuck my fingers in my ears. Still, I heard the truck door close, and I knew that my father was out there face to face with those drunk men. I squeezed my eyes shut.

Mother's voice was low and strained. "Children, sit still. Don't move."

My third brother, Daryl, started to cry as though he sensed the danger, and Mother tried to hush him by rocking him back and forth in her arms.

I heard Daddy say, "You boys step aside. We need to get through." His voice was loud and firm, the kind of voice he used on us when he wasn't standing for any monkeyshines. "I don't want any trouble. Just let us through."

I waited in agony, listening to a jumble of deep guttural sounds. They were so close I imagined I could smell their rank breath.

"Stay off our road, Preacher. Ya hear? Stay out if ya know what's good fer ya. See this here rifle ." They laughed, and it sounded like someone threw a bottle against a tree.

It seemed forever, but finally the laughter moved on across the road. I heard crashing through the dried underbrush of the woods and knew the Ashley brothers had gone. Daddy climbed back into the driver's seat, and for the first time I dared lift my head and look around. I saw the veins on Daddy's hands rigid as he gripped the steering wheel. His smile was gone, and his face was grim.

I felt as if I didn't have strength to sit up. Mother prayed out loud to thank God for His protection, and Daddy continued to drive toward the McGraw community.

I moved through the mechanics of Bible school under the tent that night, but my eyes were watching the shadows. I sang the gospel choruses, listened to the Bible stories, said my verses, and did my craft. But I was always listening for a rifle shot or looking on as the gun pointed in my daddy's face. I rode home through the woods with my head back in Jimmie's lap.

All the next day I was waiting, watching, listening for the rifle shot. Surely we would not go back to Bible school that evening. Surely we would not risk meeting drunks who stumbled from the darkness and pointed guns in our faces. It wasn't safe. Who could tell what the Ashley brothers would do?

Finally, I could stand the suspense no longer. I found Daddy out behind the house in the little log-cabin study he had built for himself. An army cot, which slept guests who came to visit, was pushed against one wall of the tiny room. The fireplace was at the far end, and Daddy's desk and file cabinet took up the third wall. Except for the door, there was nothing more to the room, only the peace and calm I always felt when I stepped inside.

Daddy was reading his Bible as he often was when I found him in his study.

"We're not going back there, are we?" I blurted out. "Aren't you scared of those men?"

I was ten years old, but I knew fear when I felt it. Daddy put down his pen and smiled. There was no hesitation on his part.

"Yes, I am a little scared, honey. We all are, aren't we? But of course we're going back. It's where God wants us."

I knew Daddy was right, but I went through the rest of the day with a hard knot in my stomach. That night we drove through the woods again. The dark stared at us as we passed, but there was no sign of the Ashley brothers that night or the rest of the two weeks of vacation Bible school. Mrs. Ashley didn't say so, but I supposed her boys were either in the woods making moonshine or had gone back to Mobile to work at the shipyards.

On the last night of Bible school, people stood around the tent, talking long after Daddy had pronounced the benediction. No one seemed to want to go home, and several people said, "Preacher, we don't remember when we've had a better school. . . ."

But I do not so easily return to the fray when I've been intimidated. I do not automatically walk back into the fire when I've been burned. My instinct is to go where the environment is cordial, warm, and affirming. Left to my feelings, I will avoid the conflict—stay out of the community when I've been threatened, choose another class when I've been attacked by the professor. My natural response is to protect my emotional comfort.

But God calls me not to emotional comfort but to obedience. I am to drive back through the woods where drunken men point guns in my face, not out of feeling but out of conviction, not because of the heart but because of the head. Risk is never a matter of the heart; it's always a matter of the will. I do not risk because I feel like it. I risk because of what God wants me to do.

But my head does not so easily take control. I am a rational creature, yes, but I am also created with glands and hormones, palms that sweat in fear and muscles that tighten in anger. What do I do with the emotional side of my nature? How do I rise above it and free myself for risk?

If I would know risk, I must confront the two sides of myself that fight for dominance. My feelings tell me to stay away from Blairston and his oral interpretation course. My reason says to complete the quarter. There are only six more weeks. I must decide whether reason or feelings will rule. If I follow feelings, where will they lead me? I will get an incomplete and will have wasted the entire quarter. Where will following my reason lead? To restoration with Dr. Blairston, at least on my part. To a grade. To the satisfied feeling that I did not run from a tough situation.

If I would learn to risk emotional discomfort, sometimes, away from the heat of the moment, I may need to stop and take a more general inventory. Do feelings or reason dictate the majority of my responses? Are my feelings keeping me from doing things I need to do, things I believe God would have me do? Is hospitable environment more important than obedience? Comfort more important than conviction?

If I would know risk, conviction must always be my criterion. I must obey whether I feel like it or not. I must drive through the woods even when I am scared. I must face Dr. Blairston even when I've been humiliated by him.

If I would know risk, I must be willing to walk without receiving positive emotional strokes from those around me. I must be willing to be unpopular with certain people, unwelcome in certain places. With Jesus, I must follow the dusty roads of Galilee toward Jerusalem, even though I know the cross awaits me there—the ultimate unwelcome.

But I do not feel like returning to Jerusalem and submitting to a cross, a crown of thorns, and a purple robe. I would rather walk where palm branches wave and the crowds shout, "Hosanna! Hosanna! Blessed is He who comes in the name of the Lord!" (see Mark 11:9).

But that's not the way of obedience. If I would risk obedience, I must "set my face resolutely toward Jerusalem." In fact, I must live my life facing Jerusalem, willing to embrace discomfort if obedience calls for it. I must walk back into situations where I am misunderstood, where harsh words may wound. I must speak up out of love and conviction when it would be easier to keep quiet and let everyone think I agree. I must honestly confront, even though it's much more comfortable to have people like me. I must be willing to return to Jerusalem, even though Jerusalem holds nothing but anguish. I must go back through the dark woods to Vacation Bible School. I must return to N14 and Professor Blairston.

It's going on noon when I open the door to N14. Dr. Blairston is alone in the room, blowing ringlets of smoke into the air and scowling into some papers on the podium.

"Dr. Blairston." I try to steady my voice.

He shifts his gaze from the papers and fixes it on me. A

look of amusement appears on his face, and he reminds me of a spider who has just caught a fly. I am still his victim. No doubt we are both remembering last Friday.

"Yes, Ms. Senter."

"Dr. Blairston, I was wondering if you'd give me another chance. I was hurt by your interrupting me last Friday, and you know I'm struggling with some of your theories. But your approval is important to me. I'd like to attempt a comeback."

For the first time I see him at a loss for words. His eyebrows go up. I've caught him off guard. Perhaps he was expecting battle. I get the feeling he is more acquainted with battle than with honesty.

Finally, he regains his composure and looks down at his gradebook.

"Well, I suppose I could erase this incomplete. How 'bout trying again on Wednesday?" His voice is almost kind.

Then as though he wants to make sure I do not think him a softy, he clears his voice, repossesses his scowl, and adds, "But I do expect better things from you."

I end up with a B on my performance of Gray's "Elegy Written in a Country Church-yard." And on the last day of class I thank Dr. Blairston for his course. He shifts nervously as though he doesn't know what to do with my thanks, then clears his throat, and says simply. "You're welcome, Ms. Senter."

Several years after graduation, I sit in a little Greek restaurant on Halstead Street and eat lunch with a professor friend from the university. We renew the years, remember people and experiences from my student days. Toward the end of the conversation I casually ask about Dr. Blairston.

Her face clouds. "Dr. Blairston killed himself two years ago in August. Found dead of gunshot wounds in his apartment. The suicide note was on his desk."

And today, years later, when I am inclined to choose the path of least resistance, to retreat from hostilities and cold receptions, I remember an angry man, standing at the point of a concrete pie-shaped classroom, accepting my honesty and my thanks. I like to think it made the torture of his life somehow easier to bear, at least for a little while. And with that thought, I find courage to return to the fray.

7

When Silence Sat in the Big Front Room

Willingness to Admit When You Have No Answers

I stand in the hall, outside my daughter's room, hesitating to awaken her this early on Saturday morning. A teddy bear smiles at me from a Love Makes Life Bearable poster hanging on her door, and the Please Do Not Disturb sign cocks itself haphazardly around the doorknob. No one pays attention to the sign. Friends and family come and go at welcomed random. Jori is a happy, good-times person, and her room, filled with posters and pictures, reflects it.

But I must open the door and bring the news that Susan has died. At age fifteen, Jori must face the awful reality of death. She will not be surprised. In some ways, we have been preparing for death ever since that bright October day, a little over a year ago, when the brain surgeon stitched up the back of Susan's head and said, "There's nothing we can do. The tumor is inoperable." Still, Jori has lived with a year and two months of hope for her friend. Maybe they will discover a cure. Maybe God will perform a miracle. Maybe the diagnosis was wrong.

Today there are no more maybes for Jori. It's over, this friendship since junior-high days. It's over, this young life so full of fun, energy, and winsomeness. I can see Susan, her long blonde hair flying behind her, running from her house to our car to join Jori for shopping, Bible study, church youth group, or piano lessons from the same teacher. Today as I open the door to Jori's room, the door has never felt so heavy.

Jori is sleeping with the blanket pulled up across her face as though to keep out the early morning sun, which is beginning to find its way between the curtains. Pictures of her friends are lined up in neat procession across the top of her bookshelves. The one of Susan in a porcelain frame with red hearts, a gift from Susan on Valentine's Day in eighth grade, is closest to her bed. Her bulletin board is layered with bits and pieces of memorabilia, tacked on as happy reminders of concerts, amusement parks, football games, trips to the beach, notes of friendship. Many are reminders of Susan—remnants of fun. Now they will also be remnants of pain.

"Jori," I say softly, almost as if I want her to sleep on. Her blanket is blue, her pillow soft. She is innocent and untouched by the world's brutalities.

She opens her eyes wide as though she already knows. "Susan?"

I nod. I cannot find any words. My eyes burn. My throat tightens. I stand helplessly by as reality hits us both. Jori turns toward the wall and pulls the blanket all the way over her head. I sit on the edge of her bed and begin to rub her shoulders.

"Please leave me alone, Mother."

"Honey, I'm so sorry. You loved Susan . . ."

"Mother, please go . . ."

Her need seems to be for time alone, but my need is to wipe her tears, hold her close, and hear her grief come pouring out. Talk about Susan, about Jori, about the two of them together, about God. I move the porcelain frame with the red hearts to the front of the bookshelf. Maybe we should look at the picture together.

There's no noise from under the blanket. She doesn't move. How can I keep quiet when my fifteen-year-old daughter has just lost one of her best friends? How can I bear not to fix it—not to give her cough syrup, a Band-Aid, or an aspirin for the pain? It's what I've always done for her before. It's what a mother is to do.

"Jori."

There's no answer.

"Jori, here's the Kleenex box for you."

There is still no answer. I know it's time to go. I've done all I can do. I've handed her the Kleenex box. I close the door. This time it closes on double grief, grief that she has lost a friend and grief that I cannot help her.

I am a stranger to grief. I've known so little. But the little I've known, I've met with words—words that relieve the pressure, words that help me know what I feel, words that help someone else know what I feel. How does one wade through grief without words?

Maybe it's my particular way, to jabber on in the face of pain. Maybe it has to do with my insecurities rearranging themselves inside. Maybe I try to fill the air so the skies don't seem so silent. That way I don't have to answer for a God who appears not to respond, a kind of human cover-up, as though God needs my words so He doesn't come across looking bad.

This morning there are no assurances and no comfort because there are no words. I cannot share Jori's grief because I am on the other side of her door. I am a stranger in a foreign land, back in the silent hall, staring at a smiling teddy bear poster. Without words, I am lost. Without words, she is alone, hiding under the blanket. Without words, there's no link. For now, I can do nothing but walk away.

During the next three days we do not talk about Susan's death; we simply live it. I pick Jori up early from school, and we drive through the brilliant October colors to the funeral home. Susan's mother is dressed in pink, and pink roses flank the parlor. I remember the day Susan and Jori shopped together for Easter dresses. Both girls came home with pink. It was "their" color.

And the rainbow was "their" symbol. They bought each other rainbow mugs and rainbow stickers for their notebooks. They even drew rainbows all over their Bible study notebooks for their after-school study with the church youth director. "They have something to do with our study of James," Jori told me one day when I asked what they meant. She would not tell me more. Only she and Susan knew for sure what the symbol meant.

Here in the funeral home, there are no rainbows, but there are pink roses. We stand before the roses with nothing to say. We hug Susan's mother and cry, still with nothing to say.

Susan's mother has brought a scrapbook from junior-high years, which rests on a table near the bank of pink roses. Jori and I turn the pages and relive the happy times when Susan was healthy and active. There's a picture of Susan's thirteenth birthday party. She and Jori are holding the pair of elephant slippers Jori gave her. Another snapshot shows the girls eating the same ice-cream cone. The caption reads: "Jori and I cool off with ice cream at Great America.

Page after page of Susan the friend with all the eighth-grade gang squeezed in around her. Susan the track star, long legs stretched out before her as she heads toward the finish line. Susan the musician in pink recital dress. Susan the honor student receiving an award.

The border of the last page is pink. A white sheet of paper with neat printing catches my eye. It's Jori's printing, and the poem is entitled "What Is a Friend?" The last line reads, "And even if our paths should part, we will be friends forever." It's sent "To Susan, With love, From Jori." I put my arm around Jori and for a moment hold her close. I feel her trembling. But still I find nothing significant to say.

Where are my words when I need them? Where are His words when I need them? They are here somewhere, I'm sure, but for now they are gagged and bound and inaccessible. I have the vague impression that I'm letting Jori down. All I can do is hand her a Kleenex box, put my arm around her, and hold her close for a moment. Even the moment is short. Fifteen-year-olds don't stand around enfolded in a mother's arms.

We walk out of the funeral home into a subdued afternoon. The colors seem muted. We meet friends in the parking lot, and the few words we exchange are hushed.

We are trying hard to understand. We are listening hard for something. . . .

———————————— ⟨⟩ ————————————

I was listening hard for something, too, as a seven-year-old sitting there on Mr. Ernest's squeaky old porch swing; listening for something more than squeaks as my brothers and I pushed ourselves back and forth. I was not sure exactly what I expected to hear. Crying? Wailing? Talking? One of my dad's sermons? Instead all we heard were squeaks from the swing. Even the front room, just the other side of the open window, was deathly quiet.

I looked through the window where Mr. Ernest's coffin rested in front of the fireplace on turquoise linoleum in a room painted bright pink. The bed had been moved out, and chairs lined the room. Almost every chair was filled and had been ever since we arrived at six o'clock that evening.

At first my brother Jimmie and I had sat on caned-bottomed chairs in the front room, dangling our legs and staring up at the picture above the mantel. It had somehow been more comforting to look at a picture of two children walking through dark woods, with a guardian angel hovering just above them, than to look at Mr. Ernest's kind old face, which now lay still and silent against white satin.

That morning, Elwood, Mr. Ernest's oldest son, had come running through the cornfield where Jimmie and I were helping Daddy pull ears of corn from the stalks and throw them on the wagon. "Preacher. Preacher Hollinger. Come quick. My daddy's done had a heart attack while he's hoeing cotton. We think he's gone."

"Ruth Ann! Turn off the motor!" Daddy yelled at me above the roar of the tractor. It had been my turn to drive the tractor, if one could call it driving. My navigational skills amounted to keeping the red Farmall's tires in the two ruts, letting out the clutch slowly when Daddy called, "Go!" and inching the tractor and wagon along the row so Daddy and Jimmie wouldn't have to throw the ears of corn so far.

I turned off the ignition. Elwood's face was red. I didn't know whether sweat or tears were dripping from his chin, and there wasn't time to decide.

"Leave the tractor here. Run tell Mother I'm going with Elwood," Daddy called back to us. He was halfway across the cornfield, dodging in and out between the cornstalks. We watched until Elwood's truck was out of sight, then ran to tell Mother the sad news. Mr. Ernest had been our friend.

We had not heard from Daddy the rest of the day, so after Mother had fried a chicken and made some rice and butter beans and we had all had our baths, we drove down the road to Mr. Ernest's house—a wide white house with a wraparound front porch. We had spent many afternoons on Mr. Ernest's front porch, drinking iced tea while my mother visited with Miz Bessie or helped her shell peas and butter beans. She always sent a sackful of goodies home with us—usually from her garden or her fruit trees.

Whenever we visited Mr. Ernest and Miz Bessie, my brothers and I went directly to the tractor tire hanging from the pecan tree in the back yard. My brother Jimmie was not very tall, but he had a strong push and could send me so high in Mr. Ernest's tire swing that I almost thought I could go right over the top of the sprawling tree.

Denny, who was only three but not one to be left out of

anything, begged until I let him climb into the swing with me. I held him tight, and Jimmie pushed harder and higher. Denny squealed when we swung and squealed when we stopped.

I thought about Mr. Ernest as we drove to his house, and parked in the front yard, and walked into the pink front room. At first I didn't want to look at him, but finally, curiosity overcame my reluctance. I slipped up to the coffin and stood by Mother and Daddy. They each had an arm around Miz Bessie who stood in the middle, looking down at her husband who just hours before had been a hard-working cotton farmer. Mother, Daddy, and Miz Bessie wiped their eyes and blew their noses. No one said anything. Daddy didn't even have his Bible. They just stood with their arms around each other and looked down at Mr. Ernest. I couldn't stand there very long. I wanted to remember Mr. Ernest alive, so I rejoined Denny and Jimmie who were sitting quietly on their chairs. Denny dropped his rubber tractor on the floor, and I picked it up and motioned for him to keep quiet.

Actually, I didn't have to tell him to be quiet. There was not a sound in the room except for occasional muffled footsteps. Neighbors and friends came through the double-front screen doors, walked down the middle hallway, deposited their food on the kitchen table, and came into the front room to look at Mr. Ernest. They hugged Miz Bessie, cried quietly into their handkerchiefs, and then sat in silence on the cane-bottomed chairs.

The mourners sat for hours, looking at the coffin, at the picture on the wall above the coffin, at the turquoise linoleum, and at their hands in their laps. They sat and said nothing. Mother and Daddy sat among them. Sometimes when people came to the door, Daddy would get up and let them in. Every now and then, he went out to the kitchen to check on Elwood and the rest of Mr. Ernest's children. But mostly, he sat quietly and waited, just like the rest of the people.

Time did not matter. Darkness came. Someone brought in two kerosene lamps and put them on the mantel. Throughout the evening, friends and neighbors kept their vigil. No words, only a sorrowful deathwatch for Mr. Ernest. No words, only their comforting presence for Miz Bessie.

At ten o'clock Mother went to each member of Mr. Ernest's family and gave a final hug. Some of the hugs took a long time. We stood patiently and waited until she had made her rounds. Daddy lifted Denny from the bed in Miz Bessie's other front room where he was sleeping and helped us to the car. Daddy would stay through the night, sitting on the hard chairs, beside Miz Bessie, her family, friends, and neighbors.

He would not say anything much, though he could because he was the preacher. He could have shared Bible verses with them or told them how hard times make strong people. He could have reminded them about all the other people he has comforted who have made it through painful times or said that Mr. Ernest was rejoicing in the presence of His Savior. It was not that Daddy had nothing to say in the face of death. But for the time being, he simply chose not to say it. His presence was more important than his words, his tears more important than answers to questions people weren't even asking.

Mr. Ernest's funeral was simple—a plain pine coffin at the altar railing of a small gray-weathered church. Someone played "Sweet By and By" on the old pump organ, and we sang "Amazing Grace! How Sweet the Sound," which was Mr. Ernest's favorite hymn. Daddy's voice was rich and deep as he read from 1 Thessalonians 4 about the dead in Christ who will rise first at the trumpet call and those who will be caught up in the air to meet the Lord. I got goose bumps on my arms and could almost imagine the angels coming down right through the roof of the little gray church and carrying Mr. Ernest into heaven right before our eyes.

Almost everyone was crying. But it seemed they were crying for the joy of heaven, not for the loss of Mr. Ernest. "Yea, though I walk through the valley of the shadow of death, I will fear no evil: for thou art with me; thy rod and thy staff they comfort me . . ." (KJV). Daddy preached the Word, and the people heard what he had to say. Maybe because he was a good preacher. Probably because they knew he loved them. Certainly because he preached God's Word. But I also think Miz Bessie, her family, friends, and neighbors heard the preacher when he did speak because my daddy knew there was a time and place to say nothing at all. . . .

———————— 🦗 ————————

But I am not so easily silenced. My natural instinct is to want to be heard. Talk impresses people with what I know and how compassionate I am. Talk is my barometer for effectiveness. I feel I have ministered if my words are smooth, ordered, and convincing. Words are indicators of my leadership, always reaching down to give others answers and advice.

But God's criterion for ministry is not how great the oration. His standard of success has nothing to do with what I say; rather, it has to do with what I am—faithful.

Ministry is sitting through the night on hard caned-bottomed chairs and sharing grief, not expounding on it. Ministry is standing by the coffin of your daughter's friend and silently handing Kleenexes to your grieving teen-ager.

If I would have courage to be silent in the face of grief, I must practice quietness in the other areas of my life as well. Sometimes I must turn the radio off, take the phone off the hook, and isolate myself in a quiet retreat center for an hour or two. If I would learn silence, I must monitor my talk. Is it necessary? Is it saying anything? Am I talking for my sake or for another's sake? Am I talking from habit? Talking to impress?

Often silence says the most. God's greatest speech was delivered in silence. On that day of crucifixion almost two thousand years ago, the earth creaked and groaned, and a rough wooden cross rose in silence from the place of the skull. The wind carried the sound of spikes on wood, the thud of a timber beam being driven into the earth, and the cries of agony, "Eloi, Eloi, lama sabachthani? [My God, My God, why have You forsaken Me?]" (Mark 15:34). In that moment when all the pain of all the ages converged on that single wooden cross-beam, heaven spoke not a word.

There could have been trumpets and angels and messages from on high, scripted in gold across the blue sky. There could have been sermons and prayers and Bible verses of promise, stained-glass chapels, organ chimes, and liturgy from rich, deep-throated voices. Yet the heavens were mute. God answered not a word, and hope was born: man's fallen world was declared redeemable. God's greatest speech was delivered in silence.

What does it mean to me, this great risk of silence? It means I am comfortable to sit here at the funeral with my daughter who grieves for her friend. I do not need to say anything or do anything. I am simply here.

The soloist begins "A Friend's a Friend Forever," a song Jori and Susan requested several times a week on the local Christian radio station call-in request program. Rick, their youth pastor, reads Jori's poem written to her friend when they were in eighth grade. I do not have the answers. I do not even have words of comfort for her.

It is risk to leave the answers at home and sit by silently. But sometimes it's the only way others can hear God speak. Sometimes it's the only way I can hear God speak. If I keep talking, I may end up with nothing to say. If I cannot hear God's voice, I have nothing to say.

Today, some years after Susan's death, the phone rings for Jori. The call is from her friend who has moved to Colorado, is depressed and thinking of leaving home. As I put the spaghetti on for dinner, I notice that Jori is not talking on the phone; she is listening. My mind goes back to pink roses, Kleenex boxes, and a silent vigil in a funeral home. Perhaps that day Jori and I were learning together. When I am inclined to respond with words, I am reminded that risking sometimes means finding the courage to say nothing at all.

8

Day of the Toboggan
Willingness to Be Needy

As February weather goes, the day is mild. A soft snow hangs onto the trees and pads the ground. We have brought sled, skates, and toboggan from off the garage wall here to Blackwell Forest Preserve, a few miles from home, to celebrate this winter day. Mark and the children are out there somewhere among the moving dots of black on white. Figures glide across the ice, hockey sticks in hand, while toboggans and sleds streak down the ridge and onto the frozen lake.

I've chosen to take the world at a slower pace—from here in the woods at the top of the hill. The world and I plod along, muffled by the layer of white. It's a good day for walking in the woods, watching the winter birds scratch for food, or sitting on a log. I survey the Currier-

and-Ives scene before me and marvel at its primitive simplicity. We are back to the basics where children breathe the pure, crisp air, roll in mounds of whiteness, and come inside with the flush of nature on their cheeks. I sense the exhilaration of the day and cannot think of a place I'd rather be in all the world than here with my family.

Mark, Jori, and Nick come panting up the hill, the sled and toboggan bobbing behind them like corks on waves. They are so buried in layers of snowsuits, hats, scarfs, and mittens I can barely see the faces that go with the voices.

"Come on, Mom. Down the hill just once with us. It's great. The snow is perfect." Jori's face is a pink glow.

Nick repeats her invitation. "Come on, Mom. You'll love it. Hardly any bumps at all." He points invitingly to the toboggan.

I remember the days, not long ago it seems, when I was the first one to the toboggan. It was fun back then, bodies piled on bodies, twisted together in a strange accumulation. Arms linked and knees bent, the wind whistled in my face, and the joie de vivre almost burst my lungs. Yes, toboggans were among the simple pleasures of life. Strange I forgot so soon.

I do not want to grow old sitting on a log at the top of a hill while my children and husband celebrate life and toboggans, I decide. I plop myself down behind the children, in number three position on the sled. Mark brings up the rear. I am comfortably protected between bodies.

"Hold tight," Jori yells from up front, and I feel the earth as it slips out from under us. We are form in motion, slicing the air with our speed, screaming with delight. Then in an instant, I realize we are off the course. We have gone wild. Out of control! The frozen lake is rushing up to meet us, and there is no ramp to ease us down. For a split second, we seem to be airborne, then we drop onto solid ice. The impact seems to push my insides right up into my head. I cannot breathe. I cannot move. I can only groan and reach toward Mark and the children as they bend over me in helpless alarm.

Nothing is clearly defined when you are in pain. A man nearby comes to help. Someone takes off my boots and makes sure I can wiggle my toes. Someone helps me get upright so I can breathe, so I can relieve the awful pressure from my back. Someone carries me up the hill, loads me into the car, and drives me to the hospital. I know my family members are in the car with me, but in my pain, they are only blurs.

The hospital corridor is wide and white. I stare up at ceiling tiles flashing overhead as the orderly pushes me toward the radiology department where x-rays will be taken. Mark and the children follow my cart like robots in a death march. I cannot maneuver myself onto the table. Someone else moves my body for me. The giant eye probes for the damage and finds it: compression break, L1 vertebra. I turn toward the wall and moan. *Dear Lord, what does it mean?* I have no idea. I only know the pain.

And the tears. I know tears here in the semidarkness of room 216. Mark and the children have long since gone home. The night nurses have given me a shot for pain and a sleeping pill for the night. Tomorrow they will rig me into traction.

Something in my back is broken, but my spirit is fractured as well. I am helpless, lying on this bed with not even the strength to raise a foot or roll over by myself. I am baggage, dependent on someone else for the most simple rudiments of life. I was undressed by an aide, lifted onto the x-ray table by lab technicians, wheeled down the hall

113

by an orderly, and rolled into bed by nurses. Two kinds of pain—physical and emotional—mix themselves together and stream down my cheeks in hot tears.

The days of pain drag by slowly. Today is day number fourteen of my hospital stay. I feel a prisoner in this bed. A steel brace holds my middle in place, and iron weights dangle from my legs. The little black "Tens Unit" box is always by my side, to be placed on the spot that hurts the most at the moment—electronics' contribution to the war against pain.

But the war I fight is also emotional. I cannot be this weak. I am strong. Independent. Self-sufficient. I do not need others very often. Mostly, they need me. It's the way I like it. Besides, what is ministry if it's not giving of myself to others? Serving. Listening. Always the hand reaching out and down to someone who depends on me. What is life if it's not coming to the end of the day with an accomplishment to hold in my hand?

Now I have been stopped short, suspended from usefulness by a runaway toboggan. I cannot move without pain, but I can clench my fist without pain, and I do. Useless. Nonproductive. Unable to keep my commitments to those who count on me. Instead, I must count on them. The nurse comes to record my temperature and blood pressure. I must let go of my clenched fist, but the battle is not so easily won.

I am still thinking about the pain of nonproductivity when Mark arrives. He stoops and kisses me on the forehead. He has brought a new *Southern Accents* magazine my friend has been supplying for me in the hospital and a plate of fresh chocolate chip cookies from Mother. She is here from Pennsylvania to be with me and care for my family. Hardly a day goes by that she does not bring or send something she has made for me. Today she even includes leftover red Valentine napkins to catch the cookie crumbs. Mark and I sip coffee and munch the cookies.

He rehearses the events of the last twenty-four hours. Mary came by with three bags of goodies for the children's lunches—enough to last a month. Shirley brought last night's dinner, Jackie picked up the ironing, Barb did the grocery shopping, and Esther and Sara are coming tomorrow to clean.

The emotional pain increases. I must get out of this bed. I must go home and see what the house looks like with all these folks coming in. I ask Mark if he would please see to it that the children straighten up their rooms, change the kitty litter, and empty the wastecans in the bathrooms before Esther and Sara come. And he might also check with the Sunshine Committee of the Sunday school class and let them know we are getting plenty of food. There's no point in someone bringing more when we have leftovers.

Mark agrees to my requests, but I suspect he knows it's more than a matter of a clean house, hot meals, and ironed clothes. "It takes courage to be needy, doesn't it?" is all he says. Then it's time for him to go, and I'm left with red Valentine napkins, chocolate chip cookies, and the struggle within. . . .

But there was no struggle by the river in a remote section of northern Arkansas. We were en route to the mountain mission station of Homing Ridge where Daddy would be conducting two weeks of evangelistic services. We had come to the end of the road, and we had to wait for the

.t was a lazy summer day, and since no ferry was in
., we decided to have a picnic, lie back on a blanket,
a. 1 look up into the blue, blue sky. The only sounds were
of the birds and the gentle lapping of the river against the
shore.

We had been on the road for almost a month, pulling an
eighteen-foot trailer behind the car. The trailer was just
big enough for a double bed for Mother and Daddy, a
closet, a sink, a refrigerator, a stove, and a table that folded
down at night into a bed for Jimmie, Denny, and me.

We were traveling during the summer months so we
could be with Daddy as he conducted evangelistic services
for small rural churches in Virginia, West Virginia, and
Arkansas. I thought it great fun to sleep in different beds,
eat different food, meet new friends, and find new ways to
cross a river.

Denny, who was three, was the only one who didn't
seem to agree that a summer of travel was great adventure.
He usually went to sleep on the hard benches some time
during Mother's flannelgraph story about *The Pilgrim's
Progress*.

But I sat wide awake and at rapt attention. Even after
hearing the stories and sermons for a month, I was caught
up with Christian and Hopeful as Mother put the colorful
figures from *The Pilgrim's Progress* on the flannelboard. I
felt my eyes get teary as she described in her gentle voice
the wonderful scene in which Christian ran toward the
cross and his heavy burden of sin finally dropped from his
back and fell into an open grave. I cringed in fear for
Christian and Hopeful when they took a short cut across
the beautiful By-path Meadow and ended up prisoners of
Giant Despair in Doubting Castle. I waited in anticipation for the last night of every revival when Mother would

describe the glorious arrival of Christian and Hopeful, across the deep river, up the steep hill, through the clouds, and into the Celestial City where they received golden crowns and praised the King forever.

Daddy's sermons didn't get old for me either. Night after night, folks came from over the hills, down in the hollows, and across the creeks to hear Daddy preach. When he gave them the opportunity to decide whether they would run their lives themselves or let God be in charge, many of them walked to the front of the church and knelt at the altar. I thought nothing could be more exciting than traveling through the country with the family and seeing people decide to follow Christ.

We finished our bologna sandwiches and began unhitching the trailer as we waited for the ferry. The folks at Homing Ridge had told us the trailer wouldn't fit on the ferry. Some said our car might not make it through the road to Homing Ridge either. Most people in those parts, we'd heard, traveled by jeep. But Daddy decided it was easier to drive the car than to take time to unload everything at the ferry. I was sorry to have missed the opportunity for a jeep ride into the mission station, but I determined that when we got there, I would travel by jeep, too.

We parked the trailer between two pine trees, far enough off the road so it would not be readily visible. Jimmie spotted the ferry coming at a snail's pace across the river. It was a barge of sorts—a wooden platform and nothing more. Two men stood at its rear and pushed with poles. As it came closer, it looked as if it was being held together with baling wire. I could understand why the people at the mission told us to leave the trailer on this side of the river.

The floating platform finally drifted ashore. There was

no ramp, so Daddy did his best to ease the car down onto the platform without dislodging its bumpers. "Easy now there, mister," the man in the red lumberman's shirt said as he guided Daddy onto the ferry.

The other man stood on shore and held onto the ferry's ropes—a human anchor, I supposed. When your ship is held together by baling wire, it's probably the only kind of anchor you can afford.

"Now ya'll keep your legs and arms out of the water," the human anchor said as we started across. "They's alligators and crocodiles in these here swamps."

His eyes twinkled down at me, and he pulled one of my braids. I had the feeling he was teasing us, but I wasn't about to take any chances. Jimmie and I climbed onto the hood of the car to watch for alligators. I would be disappointed if we didn't see one.

"Yes, sir, caught me an alligator ten foot long one time. Skinned the creature and took the skin home so my wife could have alligator shoes, though fer the life of me, can't see why no woman would want alligator shoes. Let 'em swim the rivers 'stead of wearin' 'em on your feet!"

He slapped his leg and threw back his head in laughter, a deep rumble that seemed to vibrate all the way across the river. I was sorry when our ride came to an end. The alligator man had been a great entertainer. Daddy paid for our crossing and carefully eased the car up the bank and back onto dry land.

We faced the final fifty miles of our trip into Homing Ridge, and the road on the other side of the river was everything it was described to be. The farther in and higher up we went, the narrower it became. Big boulders appeared without warning in the middle of the ruts, and at times we came so precariously close to the side of the mountain that I thought we were going to disappear for-ever among the Ozarks.

As we rode along, we looked for birds and marked down their description in the back of our bird book. Fortunately, we couldn't travel fast, so we had more time to spot the flutter of wings in the trees. Daddy had his hands full with the driving, and Denny slept peacefully on the front seat between Mother and Daddy. Watching birds and playing the "I'm thinking of someone" game made the time pass quickly. In four hours we were pulling into the mission station where the road dead-ended.

Homing Ridge, Arkansas, consisted of a church, a schoolhouse, a clinic, a gas pump, several houses clustered around the church, a house trailer or two, and a tiny cabin on the side of the hill, which would be our home for two weeks. Denny immediately saw the swings and seesaws by the schoolhouse, and Jimmie and I noted that there were plenty of rocks for climbing and woods for hiking.

We had several hours left before time for the service to begin. Jimmie and I helped Daddy unpack the car while Mother started dinner. I was carrying my suitcase into the front room, which was kitchen, living room, and my bed-room all in one, when I noticed Mother holding her stom-ach and leaning over the sink. Her face was white, and her lips looked dried and shriveled.

"Run get Daddy," she managed to say in a faint voice.

I dropped my suitcase and ran down the hill toward the car. By the time Daddy and I got back, Mother was lying on the couch. Daddy felt her forehead and was sure she felt hot. Together we led her to the back bedroom and helped her get undressed. Daddy told her not to worry about din-ner or the service. *The Pilgrim's Progress* would wait until she felt better. I was disappointed that Mother would miss the first night of services, but she assured me that she would probably be up and around after a good night of sleep. Maybe it was just the long trip over bumpy roads.

When we came back from the service, Daddy took Mother's temperature. It was 103 degrees. I got her ice water from the refrigerator, and Daddy brought cold wash-cloths for her face. Then we knelt around her bed, on the cold, drafty floor, and prayed if it was God's will, she would soon be well. I lay awake for a long time in my couch-bed under the window and listened to the night sounds and thought about my mother. She hardly ever got sick, and now that she was, everything seemed at loose ends. I tried to believe she would be better in the morning.

But morning came, and Mother was not better. She was worse. She kept her eyes closed and barely moved when I went in to talk to her. She had not eaten since our picnic the previous day. Daddy tried to give her ginger ale, but it wouldn't stay down. By midafternoon, Mother was still vomiting, and her temperature had climbed to 104. Daddy went to the clinic to see the nurse.

The nurse in her crisp white uniform was back up the hill with Daddy in no time, carrying a doctor's bag. She was not a doctor, but when I had met her last night at the service, someone said she was the only "doctor" in a hundred miles. At any rate, I knew she was a very busy lady. But she seemed happy to see if she could do anything for Mother.

"We need to be careful about dehydration," she said to Daddy in a low voice when she came back into the front room. "We have to keep trying to keep the fluids down. I'll check back with you later tonight."

I stayed close by Mother for the rest of the day, filling her glass with ice, rinsing out the washcloth for her forehead with cold water, making sure the covers were tucked in around her feet, and trying to keep Denny happy and quiet. I heard her tell Daddy she was sorry about the Bible classes she was supposed to have taught every morning in the schoolhouse and the children's lessons for the evening services.

"We just want you to get well," Daddy said. "Forget about what you were supposed to do."

By the next morning, word had spread around the station and out into the mountains: the evangelist's wife was sick. Bright and early, someone knocked on our cabin door with a basket of hot biscuits and fresh blackberry preserves. Before long, another lady stopped by with some fresh flowers and a little book of prayers for Mother to read. Throughout that day and for the rest of the two weeks, while Mother remained in bed, people came to our door bringing meals—vegetables from their gardens, fruit from their trees, canned goods from their shelves, and hot biscuits, cakes, and pies from their ovens.

We hardly knew their names, but they came through the side door of the cabin, put their offering on the table, tiptoed quietly into my mother's room, and told her how glad they were she and Daddy had come to Homing Ridge. Mother was weak and tired, but she smiled, reached out her hand, and said a simple, "Thank you." I never once heard her tell anyone, "You really don't have to do this for us. We are managing fine."

The nurse came up the hill twice a day to check on Mother. She had many patients to see, but she always took time to chat as she took Mother's temperature, checked her blood pressure, or gave her a shot for nausea. Some days the nurse even took time to change the sheets on the bed. Another day, she took Denny back to the clinic so

Mother could get some uninterrupted sleep. And when she felt Mother needed a stronger medication, she sent a jeep over the mountain fifty miles to get some.

The two weeks came and went. Daddy preached every night, taught Bible classes each morning, and visited the mountain folk in the afternoons. The little church at the bottom of the hill was filled every night, and every night after the song service, the people knelt and prayed for Sister Hollinger, Brother Elam's wife.

By the end of the two weeks, the medicine brought in by jeep had begun to work, and the nurse thought Mother would be well enough to travel. The evangelistic meetings had ended, and Mother hadn't taught one Bible lesson or given one children's message. In fact, she hadn't even made it out of bed to one of the services. Yet Mother had ministered to the people of Homing Ridge in another way. She had allowed them to serve her.

As we loaded the Dodge for the long haul back over the mountain, one by one the people came, hugged my mother, and thanked her for her ministry to them. They stood in a group by the schoolhouse and waved good-bye to us as long as we could see them. I saw Mother wiping tears from her eyes. Those people had become her dear friends, even though all she had had strength to say to them was, "Thank you." Maybe that was why they had become such good friends in such a short time. . . .

———————————— 🦛 ————————————

But I do not find it easy to be needy. I would rather be strong, independent, and able to control the details of my life. I live in a world that honors strength and productivity, that worships power and plans. By nature, I think of my value in terms of my contributions more than in terms of the quality of my life.

Even when it comes to faith, I must do the work of the faithful. I must minister to the needy and be strong for the weak. I must be forever working toward my goals, crossing off items on my agenda, attending this meeting or that, tackling this new project, meeting this deadline, and fulfilling this obligation. And the more I do for the Lord, the more effective I suppose myself to be.

But the path to risk is not so. Risk taking doesn't grow from strength. It grows from a willingness to be weak and to trust God anyhow. If I would learn about risk, I must learn about weakness. I must allow myself the courage to ask for help, to let others serve me, to be the learner rather than always the teacher, and to be humble enough to receive as well as to give. I must open wide my doors and let people bring me food, clean my bathrooms, change the sheets on my bed, and teach my Bible lessons for me.

Even as I lie in bed with a broken back, I think about this risk of weakness. *Why do I want to be able to do it all myself? So that others can stand back at a distance and admire my strength? So that I don't have to humble myself and admit I am not capable of doing it myself? So that I don't have to run the risk of inconveniencing someone else? So that I can have the personal satisfaction of seeing results for my day?*

If I would truly minister, I must be willing to minister from weakness, for then there is no doubt about whose glory is being demonstrated. I must see myself as a creature of need, not of power. I must sit with Paul in Philippi, as he scribbles a message to the church in Corinth. I am their leader, but I must let them know "most gladly I will rather boast in my infirmities, that the power of Christ may rest upon me. . . . I take pleasure in infirmities. . . .

For when I am weak, then I am strong" (2 Cor. 12:9–10). I must embrace eye infirmities, shipwrecks, harassment, jail, warrants of arrest. I must be at peace with a broken back. For paradox of all paradoxes, I am not truly strong until I have been weak.

My hospital stay behind me, I have returned home. Judy stops at my bedroom door with a basket of fruit. I have often seen her and spoken to her, but she is always an arm's length away, our relationship nothing more than polite formalities. But now, she arranges the basket beside my bed and pulls up a chair. It is as though we are two disabled people helping each other across the street. My weakness somehow opens a door in Judy. Perhaps it is that we are both vulnerable together. She asks about my accident and talks about some of her own private pain. And when she stands to leave at the end of the hour, she says simply, "It's nice to know you have needs too."

I wonder why she has come, but I sense ministry has taken place in this very room—the ministry that happens when two people are willing to need each other. The legacy of a broken back will live for years to come, spurring me to surrender my strength again and again, returning me to my place of need.

9

Who Is This Dinner Guest Really?

Willingness to Move Beyond Categories

Yellow daffodils seem appropriate to the day—bright, cheerful, full of sunshine. I arrange them in a crystal vase and set them in the middle of the dining-room table. They are the spring I covet, and even though they came from the grocery store and not my garden, they hold promise of blooms to come.

February is too much like life. One day follows another in endless monotony of gray and cold. Celebrations of holidays are too long ago to remember, and the rites of spring are too far in the future to hope for. I am stuck with humdrum. I roam through the month like a caged animal with instincts for open grassland. But I must endure February to get to March when I can feel alive again.

Today there is hope. With the sun streaming through

the windows and yellow daffodils on the table, how can I resent February? I glance at the kitchen clock. The chicken is in the oven for dinner, and it's time to pick up Jori from school. Small events seem like festivities today. Tomorrow the gray days will return.

Meanwhile, we will enjoy daffodils and entertain Royce for dinner tonight. He has become a frequent guest. I simply add an extra piece of meat to the pan and bring out the good dishes for the dining-room table, and we have instant extended family. No bother or elaborate preparations. Royce is just Royce. He isn't the kind of person to evoke a lot of fuss, although he hardly ever appears at our door without flowers or candy for the cook and a toy or two for the children.

Life is sometimes strange in the unlikely combinations it puts together. Royce is city; we are suburban. He has spent most of his life in academics; we, in ministry. He is into sports cars; we drive a Chevy Vega station wagon. His clothes come from Burberry's on Michigan Avenue; we shop the outlets.

As class rosters went, he and Mark were next to each other in a doctoral course at the university. They had talked before class, shared breaks, and participated together in comprehensives study groups, but other than that, Royce had been an associate in academics, nothing more.

Then he and Mark bumped into each other, several years later, in the stacks of a local junior college library. He was on an educational assignment in the suburbs. Since it was almost dinner time and Royce had no plans, Mark invited him home. Later that evening, when Mark asked about his family, he said he had no family anymore.

"Wife and kids have gone back East. It's better that way, but I do miss my children." I could hear the longing in his voice and see it in the way he sat on the floor and rolled a ball back and forth to two-year-old Nicky.

Royce was the kind of person you sat and listened to long after dinner was over. He had stories about politics in Chicago's Forty-third Ward that made even six-year-old Jori sit spellbound. He had been to Turkey, sailed a catamaran through the Great Lakes, and attended regularly at the Bahai House of Worship. Religion was one of Royce's favorite topics, and it often found its way into our conversations. Royce was open to our views and seemed knowledgeable about the Christian faith, but only as an academic pursuit, not as a way of life.

If there were struggles in Royce's life, they did not appear on the surface. But one morning, Royce called and asked for Mark's phone number at the office. He had always called Mark at home, after work. I hoped there were no emergencies.

"Royce is having a rough time right now," Mark said when he came home from work later that evening. "He dropped by the office this morning. We talked for several hours. The guy is really hurting."

I was not surprised that Royce was having some tough times, especially with his family gone. I didn't press for more information. What Mark learned about a person through counseling was private, and if he ever felt he needed to share information with me in confidence, he did. Otherwise, we trusted each other and didn't bother about it.

Royce continued to come for dinner when he could, and even more often, he dropped by to talk with Mark at the office. I enjoyed his times in our home, was happy we could share our family with him, and felt confident about the help Mark was able to give him.

And so I set the table tonight for dinner and think about the last year since Royce and Mark got reacquainted in the library stacks. Mark tells me Royce is doing very well in his career and has been traveling a good bit lately. Conversationalist that he is, Royce doesn't tell us much about his personal life. For all the times he has been to dinner, there are still large blocks of unknowns about him. He is much more willing to talk abut his prophet Bahaullah and the writer Saul Bellow than about himself. One of the refreshing things about him is his willingness to talk about lots of subjects; he doesn't always need to talk about himself.

Royce arrives at six with a box of chocolate truffles. He looks like an ad fresh off the pages of *Gentlemen's Quarterly* with his three-piece suit and his Burberry trench coat with red-and-tan lining.

"Seems like a long time since you've been here, Royce. Glad you could come tonight." I take the box of candy and hang his coat in the front hall closet.

"It has been a while. Lots of things have been keeping me on the run lately," he answers. He makes himself at home in the living room among the toys, the children, and the evening newspaper.

I mean to ask what he's been doing, but my timer goes off in the kitchen and Mark comes in from his office at church. The question will have to wait until later.

As I sit at the dinner table and watch the candlelight play on the daffodils, I wonder, *What brings people together and keeps them together long after any apparent reason for togetherness has ceased?* We have so little in common with this citizen of the world who has just flown in from business in San Francisco. What business, I am not sure. He apparently does not need to impress us with the facts.

Instead, he tells us about a Ved Mehta work, *Mahatma Gandhi and His Apostles*, he has just finished reading. He claims with great certainty that of the more than four hundred Gandhi biographies so far written, this is by far the best. I would not be surprised if he has read all four hundred, but I don't ask.

The children have finished eating and have gone off to play in their rooms. Besides the Ved Mehta work, we have discussed the latest breakthrough in genetic engineering, recombinant DNA techniques, and the political summit in London.

We have just begun Chicago politics when I notice it's time to put the children to bed. Royce once told us he had some political aspirations. I'm interested in exactly what he has in mind, but I excuse myself anyhow and set about the evening rituals—pajamas pulled on, teeth brushed, story told, prayers said, hugs and kisses shared, nightlights turned on, and doors closed. "Night, Mommie . . . Night, Mommie . . . Night, Mommie . . ." It's Nicky's way of prolonging the ritual and avoiding bedtime for another minute or two.

I'm returning to the kitchen for more coffee when I hear the words: "Now that I've come out of the closet . . ." I'm glad I haven't yet picked up the coffeepot. I don't think I could hold it steady, much less pour. I pretend to do something at the sink. The pieces fall together in an instant. His wife in the East. "It's better that way." Frequent trips to San Francisco. The "cause" I've heard him talk about without going into detail. The counseling sessions with Mark. I turn on the hot water tap and let it splash full blast into the sink. I can't think of anything else to do.

Royce is a homosexual! Certainly Mark knew. He has probably known for a while. And he didn't tell me. He kept inviting Royce into our home, to be with our children, to eat at our table. It's as though my brain is on overload and can't decide what to do with the information.

Do I go back to the table and pretend I haven't heard? Do I stay in the kitchen and wash the dishes until he leaves? Do I pour the coffee, smile pleasantly, and ask about his political aspirations? I don't even care about his aspirations anymore. His family. Him. All I want is to cut off this relationship as quickly as possible, like in fifteen minutes. Say good-bye and let him go his way. Some differences don't matter. This one does.

The hot water steams up from the sink and splashes over the counter. I stare into the dark outside and watch as the headlights of a car start down our street. I am standing watching them come toward our house. . . .

I watched headlights coming toward me once long ago in our little white church among the Alabama pines. But it wasn't just a single pair of headlights. A long snakelike gleaming caravan twisted its way around the curve where the road turned at the grocery store. That monster creeping toward us in the night was an awesome sight. I didn't know exactly what to make of it, but I had heard rumors about recent Ku Klux Klan activities, and I was afraid my worst fears were about to be confirmed.

Daddy sat calmly behind the pine pulpit, just under the gold-framed picture of Christ weeping over Jerusalem. He joined in heartily as we sang, "When the roll is called up yonder I'll be there . . ." I knew he could see the approaching lights. I was also certain he knew what they meant.

Once before, at revival services in another church, I had seen the Klan. They had appeared out of the dark, like ghosts from a graveyard. Daryl, number three of my four brothers, who was three at the time, had screamed so hard my mother had to take him to a neighbor's house to quiet him down. I hadn't screamed, but I had felt like it. White-hooded figures were everywhere in the churchyard. Jimmie, Denny, and I had run shaking to Daddy.

"They are the Ku Klux Klan," Daddy had whispered to us. "They won't hurt us. We probably know the people under those hoods. They are not here to cause trouble for any of us."

I thought he emphasized the "us," but I didn't understand who the others were until several years later when a black state-road worker and his family moved into the foreman's house three miles down the road. He was to supervise the new interstate and was the only black for miles around.

The black family moved in one day and out the next. Daddy drove us down the road to see the bullet holes in the front door.

"This is what happens when people hate" was all Daddy said. We stood there for a long time and stared at the empty house with holes in the front door. No one said anything—no one had to. But I dreamed of bullets in the night, and every time we drove down the road past the foreman's house I thought about hate.

Only six months later, I sat in our church and watched the headlights come toward us. My church had always meant security and love. The cement block walls were painted a soft green and broken by knotty pine boards along the front wall to make the platform area different from the rest. Four gas heaters—two at the front and two at the back—kept us warm in winter, and cardboard fans on sticks cooled us in the summer. The antique Chickering piano—a gift from a wealthy businessman somewhere— looked terribly out of place in our little country church. It sat proudly to the left of the platform where it blocked all but the slightest passageway into the back Sunday school room. Mother sat on the round piano stool and played as though nothing out of the ordinary were happening. I suddenly wished I were sitting beside her rather than three-fourths of the way back beside two of my friends who did not promise much in the way of protection. One was smaller than I and probably even more scared.

I remembered the bullet holes in the foreman's house down the road. Why were the Klan coming to our church? What would they do?

"They won't hurt us," Daddy had said when we had seen them at the other church. Later, he had told us the Klan often showed up at churches to remind the community that they were around. They did not cause disturbances and were each required to give a dollar in the offering plate. I was glad about the offering, but white hoods in the night were a fearful sight and I wished they had not picked our church.

We went on singing, "What a friend we have in Jesus. All our sins and griefs to bear . . ." I think we sang more loudly than usual to cover up our nervousness. The caravan of lights began to turn into our churchyard. Over the music, I heard doors slamming. None of the trucks had pulled in very close to the building—maybe so we couldn't identify them.

I couldn't recognize anyone as the procession of white started down the aisle by twos. All I could see were shoes sticking out from underneath the robes. Once I dared look up into a pair of eyes peering through slits in a hood. I was so frightened by the sight of all the white figures that I buried my face in my songbook again.

Daddy motioned for the people sitting on the left side of the church to move across the aisle, leaving the whole left side vacant. The ghostly parade filed into vacated pews and stood at attention until the last member was in place. Then they sat down in unison.

I wondered how Daddy felt standing up in front, looking into fifty pairs of mystery eyes. If he was afraid, he didn't show it.

"We want to welcome our visitors tonight," Daddy said as though he genuinely meant it. "We hope you will feel the love that is in this place." Mother smiled over toward the Klan side of the church as she finished at the piano and took her seat on the front row.

All the way through the sermon I thought about burning crosses and bullet holes. I didn't hear much of what Daddy was saying. I was too busy hoping Klansmen liked sermons that included the word *love*. Since Daddy was preaching from 1 John, he couldn't avoid it. I wondered, too, what they would do if they didn't approve. Daddy preached with his normal gentle power, calling his congregation "beloved," smiling down on the delegation in white, and looking them squarely in the eye. I somehow felt he had as much compassion for the men in white as for his own flock.

When he had pronounced the benediction, he walked to the back door to greet worshipers as usual. We stood in place and watched as the delegation filed out. Each one stopped at the door, greeted the preacher, and dropped a dollar bill into a basket on the table. I noticed Daddy spoke personally to the men. I wondered if he knew who they were. If he did, I was certain he would never tell us their identity.

I heard truck motors start up and watched out the window as the caravan crawled back around the curve and into the night. We stood around and talked for a while about our visitors. Miz Roberts said she was sure they hadn't come to make any trouble and we probably wouldn't have an official visit from them again. She complimented Daddy on welcoming them so kindly. "Yet you still preached about love," she added. "Some preachers won't do that, you know. Lots of preachers are just plain scared of 'em."

Daddy left to take a truckload of people home, and I waited until Mother had finished talking so I could walk with her across the churchyard to our house. I didn't want to walk it alone. Once safely inside, I looked from the living-room window every few minutes to make sure no caravans were coming back. I finally relaxed when Daddy pulled into the yard and the curve in the road remained dark. We were all safe, and more important, Daddy and Mother had opened their arms to people they strongly disagreed with. I knew Daddy would continue to talk about what hate can do, but that night, he had distinguished between person and act. He had embraced the person without embracing the cause.

The next day when I came home from school and told Daddy that Julia May had seen Mr. Maze's truck in our yard last night during church, Daddy looked serious and said, "Ruth Ann, try to forget what Julia May said. Mr. Maze is your bus driver and friend."

I never did find out whether Mr. Maze was really one of the men in white or not, but the next week, just about sunset one evening, Daddy took us fishing at Mr. Maze's pond as he often did. He stood for a long time at the pasture gate and talked to Mr. Maze, his friend and neighbor. . . .

Yet as an adult, I struggle to get beyond the categories. My inclination is to think of people by their associations—ethnic and radical groups, socioeconomic status, church affiliation, lifestyle, or geographic distinctions. I am quick to lump together those of a certain kind and assume that what is true of one is true of the other. Even more unfairly, I often consent to the labels glibly applied by an undiscerning, unloving world.

My natural inclination is to stay with those of my kind and to avoid members of a group I do not understand or agree with. Something in my attitude toward Royce changed the minute I found out he was a homosexual. He is still the same person. I did not fear him before or feel he was contaminating our home. I looked at him as a person Mark and I enjoyed, a person with needs, an individual for whom Christ died. Now I want him out of my house forever.

But if I would be free to risk, to grow, I must move beyond the categories and love across the barriers for Christ's sake. I must face the stereotypes I have created for people and deal with my oversimplified groupings—my quick judgments of those of another kind. I must check the mental images I have drawn up for people and concentrate on the person rather than on the accessories. The color of their skin, how much money they make, and the kinds of people they associate with are side issues. The real issue concerns who they are as individuals and their standing before God.

If I would learn to risk associations with those unlike myself, I must lay aside my need for approval and understanding. I must sit with Jesus at Simon's table where a prostitute from town comes and pours expensive perfume over my feet. I must permit this woman, who violates everything I stand for, to wash my feet, dry them with her hair, and cry over me so that tears and perfume together trickle down my feet.

It is unlawful, unclean, unheard of, for a sinner, much less a woman, to touch a rabbi. She has crashed the party, intruded into a gathering of the religious power base. I have a reputation to protect. I can't give room for scandal in plain view of the Pharisees. I must play it cool. Keep my sacred distance. Let others know where I stand when it comes to the social illnesses of the day. Mow down the people as well as their ungodly causes. It's too much trouble to separate the sin from the sinner anyhow. Cut them all off, and I'll be safe. And safety is what is important.

But if I would risk as Jesus risked, I must stand with courage in defense of the one who does not exactly fit the prescribed mold. I must point to her strengths and say to the skeptics looking on, "She loved much" (Luke 7:47). I must see her for what she could be, not what she is at the moment: "Your sins are forgiven" (Luke 7:48). I must consider her needs and extend to her the resources of God that have been given to me: "Your faith has saved you. Go in peace" (Luke 7:50). If I would be free to grow through risking, I must touch the world where it hurts and leave the consequences with God.

The hot water continues to splash in my kitchen sink, and I have had time to think. It's dark outside, and February has returned. Even the yellow daffodils have lost their pleasure. But they are still in the middle of the table next to the empty coffee cups. The daffodils are not contaminated. My dinner table is not contaminated. I am not contaminated. My husband is my husband, bent on serving God and others. What do I have to fear from this one, so different and yet so like us in our need for divine enablement?

I fear for him, his future on the road he has chosen. I fear for his wife and children and for all who follow his course. But fear for him and fear for myself are different matters. Fear for him should move me toward him, with more chicken dinners and yellow daffodils and cups of hot coffee. Fear for myself is bound to move me into my shell of protection until all that is left is a vase full of yellow daffodils in February with no one around my table who needs them.

I turn off the hot water tap, wipe up the splashes, and return to the table with the coffeepot and the oatmeal cookies. At first, I can't bring myself to look directly at Royce. I'm still struggling. But I have poured the coffee and served the cookies. I'm on my way across the barrier.

Years have passed since Royce last sat at our table. He continued to drop in for dinner now and then as long as he lived in the area. For years after he moved to another part of the country, we received a note every Christmas with a check included. "For your kindness and love to me," it often read. One year he wrote, "Sometimes I think you two are the only sane people I know."

We do not know what has happened to Royce. Several years ago his notes stopped coming, and our cards to him were returned with "Address unknown." But today when I am tempted to draw my cloak of righteousness close around me to keep from contamination, I remember daffodils in the middle of a dining-room table and notes at Christmas. In that memory I somehow find courage to embrace the person even when I disagree with the cause.

10

Crazy Man Braggett Lives Down This Road

Openness to Change

Life without change would be like a year without the seasons—no passages, no growth, and no tender young sprouts in the spring. But sometimes change comes, and like a snowstorm in April, it catches you off guard. Today I'm not prepared for Jori's request.

"Mother, the sign outside the pool says when you are nine you can go swimming alone. May I go by myself today?"

We are munching lunchtime potato chips on the patio when she asks. So far the day has been routine, the summertime schedule of no rush or bother. I have pulled weeds in the garden this morning and put impatiens plants along the side of the house. Nicky has been beside me, digging in the dirt and making roads for his Matchbox trucks. Jori, with her Nancy Drew book, has been off on some mystery adventure launched from the hammock hanging between two trees in the back yard. It's the way I like mothering. Close and within earshot.

Going to the pool has always been a family outing. A short rest time after lunch, then pack our beach bag, and ride our bikes down the street and around the corner to the park district, a community hub of summertime fun. I keep my eye on the children, read or do paperwork from my lounge chair in the sun, and revel in this ritual of togetherness and relaxation.

Now Jori is asking to go alone. I'm secure enough to know it's not a vote against me but a small plea for independence—a faint stretching of her personhood. But should it come so soon? She is only nine. She swims, but does she swim well enough? She is careful on her bike, but is she careful enough? She knows the neighbors for blocks around, but is she discerning at age nine?

She stands before me today, so much a child yet a budding adult. I have every reason to trust her. I know I cannot squeeze the adult part of her back through the cracks. I must let it come out a little at a time.

After a long, thoughtful pause, I answer, "Yes, Jori. You may go alone. Don't forget your towel and pool pass. The beach bag is on the washer."

End of one ritual. Beginning of a new. I tuck Nicky in for his nap and walk with Jori to the end of the driveway. She has remembered everything, even a quarter from her bank to buy an ice-cream cone. I feel the need to rehearse all I've been teaching her in the last nine years, but she obviously has one thought on her mind: getting to the pool. I decide if she hasn't heard it in the last nine years, she will not hear it today. I cut the rehearsal and remind her I will expect her home at three o'clock. She is off in a flash, white beach shirt billowing behind her. At the corner she turns and waves, then disappears behind a house.

Once back in the kitchen, I go through the motions of washing the lunch dishes, but mostly I am at the pool, locking my bike, finding a locker for the beach bag, taking the first dive off the board, buying ice cream, and talking with friends. Strange thing, this mothering, you are mentally in two places at once: where you are and where your children are.

At one o'clock I settle into some paperwork at my desk. I wonder how things are going at the pool. Two o'clock and Nicky awakens from his nap. We eat popsicles out on the patio, and I watch as he rides his three-wheeler around the yard. I wonder about Jori. Two-thirty. A police siren wails from the direction of the pool. I look west toward the park district, but all I can see are the blue spruce and pine trees in our neighbor's yard.

Things are different now. As of today, she goes to the pool alone. I have vested my confidence in her. I cannot take it back. Nicky and I read on the front porch swing until I see Jori's little blue bike turn the corner. She waves when she spies us and rides up the driveway with a big smile on her face. It's three o'clock on the dot. "Did you miss me?" she asks as she props her bike against the porch step.

"Yes, Jori. I missed you a lot."

She seems satisfied to know. Now she can tell me about her big adventure and she does—everything from seeing Mrs. Fromer in her back yard to the kind of ice-cream bar she bought. It's a proud moment for her, simple as the moment may be—a small but significant passage for both mother and daughter. Tomorrow the good-byes will be more painful. The older she gets, the more I will have to lose. But the small good-byes today prepare me for the more difficult ones tomorrow.

Years go by, with their share of passages, changes, and small and large good-byes. I never quite get used to them. It's spring, and Jori is just a few months from turning sixteen.

I hear the car door slam, and the front door bursts open. "Mom. Guess what! I've been invited to Aruba for the summer! They want me to work at the radio station."

Aruba! I know nothing about it except it is home base for some college friends who manage a missionary radio station there. They have invited Jori to be their guest for the summer. We look for Aruba on the world globe that sits on Nicky's desk. It's an island so tiny we can't even find it. One paragraph in *The World Book Encyclopedia* defines the country: "Aruba: A group of West Indian islands just off the coast of Venezuela. It covers 75 square miles. Its population is about 65,000. It is a refining center for crude oil shipped from Venezuela."

There is something unsettling about the thought of handing over your child to a place you do not know—a place that barely takes up a paragraph in the encyclopedia and has no space on the globe. I am also handing her over to that vast, impersonal system out there called travel. Lines at the airport. Unpredictable weather patterns in the sky. Mechanical variables. Customs agents. International configurations. It's a system overwhelming enough for veteran travelers, but for a sixteen-year-old?

My mind is full of unanswered questions as we sit down to dinner. To say good-bye for a week of summer camp or a visit to Grandma's house in Pennsylvania is one thing. But a summer in Aruba?

"So what do you think, Mom and Dad?" Jori reintroduces the topic when dinner is over.

"I don't know, Jori. I'm just not sure about this one. . . ."

I had heard similar words before, years ago when another mother struggled with change and relinquishment. "I don't know, Ruth Ann. Daddy and I will have to talk about it," my mother said in her gentle tone.

I sat at the kitchen table after school, drinking milk and eating cookies. I wanted very badly to go home from school with Mary Margaret on Thursday and spend the night at her house. She had invited me as soon as she had gotten to school that morning. Her mother had said it would be fine.

Mary Margaret's mother drove the school bus and worked in the school cafeteria. She was a very sweet lady and often asked about my mother and daddy when I went through the lunch line. Since Daddy was president of the PTA, he and Mother knew most of the school workers. It wasn't that I'd asked to visit complete strangers.

I had never seen Mary Margaret's house, but she lived in the Bartlett community where Douglas Dawes lived. Since he was my present second-grade crush, I thought riding Mary Margaret's bus would be very nice. Besides, Mary Margaret was my friend, and friends in my class spent the night with each other all the time. I didn't bother to tell Mother about Douglas. I wasn't altogether sure the information would help my cause.

Later that evening as I undressed for bed, Mother came to my room. "Daddy and I think it will be okay for you to go home with Mary Margaret Thursday after school. Be sure and thank Mrs. Jerkins. It's awfully kind of her to invite you."

Thursday morning I was ready for school thirty minutes before the bus came. My little blue train case was packed and waiting by the door. "And dear Lord, please take care of Ruth Ann as she goes to visit Mary Margaret. May she carry Your joy with her to that home," Mother prayed at the breakfast table.

When it was time for the school bus, she kissed me good-bye and walked with Jimmie and me to the gate; then she stood waving as the bus pulled away. Mother never walked us halfway to the school bus. I was somewhat embarrassed but also secretly glad Mother cared when I went away. Maybe my going to Mary Margaret's house wasn't as easy a decision for her as I had thought.

That day at school seemed endless. Finally, the last bell rang, and I grabbed my train case and scurried with Mary Margaret toward bus number two. It seemed strange to be going to the front of the bus line instead of the back. But then, everything would be different for the rest of the day. I had no idea how different.

I didn't remember ever having been on the road between our school and Bartlett. We were hardly a mile from school when the road began to look like someone had hit it with a sledgehammer. The big yellow bus creaked and groaned across the pits in the middle of the road. Mary Margaret's mother shifted into a lower gear, and we lunged sharply to the left. I almost wished someone would suggest we walk across the pits, but no one else seemed to notice. In fact, everyone talked and laughed noisily, as if yawning pits in the middle of the road were everyday occurrences.

The road finally leveled, but we had no sooner gotten

on firm ground than we faced the wash—a swampy bog that branched from the creek farther up. There was no bridge. Why build a bridge when a light vehicle could go through the wash without one? If the load was too heavy, the passengers just took off their shoes and socks and walked across.

"Hurry, Ruth Ann. We've got to get out and walk." Mary Margaret was halfway out the door without her shoes before I understood what was happening. I thought it great adventure to walk across a bog with my shoes off until I felt the slime and rocks on the bottom. Someone behind me threw a stick and yelled, "Snake!" I screamed and almost fell, but Mary Margaret grabbed me.

"Don't worry, Ruth Ann. They's just teasing you."

I was relieved when we were back in the bus and on our way again. I was beginning to think how nice my bus run was. We had bumpy dirt roads, but at least we didn't have pits and slimy washes. I wondered if Mother and Daddy knew how bad the road to Bartlett was.

The sun was almost beneath the trees when we got to Mary Margaret's house, a small square with a door in the middle and two wooden shuttered windows on each side. I had forgotten that if your mother drove the school bus, you were the last one to get off. The house was not painted, and I noticed some of the boards near the roof were dangling. An old rusted-out shell of a car sat in the front yard, and we walked by the woodpile where a man who must have been her daddy was chopping logs. He grunted some sort of greeting as he swung the ax and brought it down hard against the pine. Crack! Splinters flew everywhere. "Go get the woodbox and come pick up these here chips," he yelled at Mary Margaret.

"But I have a friend . . . ," Mary Margaret started to protest but stopped herself midsentence. "Yes, sir," she said meekly and went for the kindling box.

We picked up the pine chips, which would no doubt be used to start the evening fire. Her father continued to swing his ax with a vengeance. A scar across the side of his face made him look like he was always scowling. I was just as glad when we had finished our job and could move away from him.

Mary Margaret's house had one long room on the left and two smaller rooms on the right. We went into the big room, which was bedroom, sitting room, and kitchen combined into one. Mary Margaret asked if I would like some buttermilk and cornbread. I wondered if that was to be dinner or an after-school snack, but I didn't ask.

"Sure," I answered as enthusiastically as I could. I had never drunk pure buttermilk, although I knew the smell. The first swallow had to be the worst. I decided if I didn't breathe while I drank it, I wouldn't smell or taste it either. I drank the whole glass of buttermilk without breathing, and my head started to pound from holding my breath. But the buttermilk was down, and the cornbread covered up the taste.

Mary Margaret took a basket off the wall and said we had to deliver milk and eggs down the road to her grandpa who lived alone and couldn't get out anymore. I thought a walk down the road sounded like fun.

I pulled my pink jacket closer around me as we started through the front yard. It was amazing how dark it had gotten in such a short time. I was hoping her grandpa didn't live too far down the road, but I couldn't see any other houses from Mary Margaret's front yard.

"It's not a very far piece," Mary Margaret said as though

she had read my mind. I was carrying the basket of eggs, and she held tightly to the bucket of milk with a cloth across its top. The wind was beginning to filter its night breezes through the tops of the pines as though striking a minor chord. I had a growing sense of eerieness. But if we walked fast, we would get home fast, I reasoned. Mary Margaret was almost running to keep up with me, and I decided for the sake of the eggs, I'd better slow down.

I always enjoyed walking beneath the pines, but Mary Margaret's part of the woods seemed somehow deeper than ours. *How could things be so much different just twelve miles away from home?* I wondered.

"See that house over there?" Mary Margaret pointed to a brown-shingled house that looked like a pile of forsaken bones to me. The only sign of life was smoke coming from the chimney. "Crazy Man Braggett lives there. He doesn't cut his hair, and his fingernails are that long." She apparently gave me a visual distance, but I couldn't see through the dusk and I didn't bother to look. "Some say he's even killed some people, but he's never given us no trouble and I've lived here all my life. I think he's about eighty-five years old. I see him in his yard sometimes. Don't think he'd be out this time of day."

I was somewhat relieved, but not much. I forgot about the eggs and picked up speed again. We seemed to be running a race with the dusk. Grandpa's house was just beyond the bend in the road, and I was comforted to see a dim light in the front window.

We said hello to Grandpa who was sitting in a big chair by the front-room window, and we put the basket of eggs in the pie safe and the milk on the back porch shelf where it would be cool overnight.

"Can't y'all sit a spell?" Grandpa asked, but Mary Margaret told him we wanted to get home before dark. I agreed with her about getting home. I wasn't really afraid; I was just ready for the adventure to be over.

We were passing the crazy man's house when a dark furry creature scurried across the road in front of us. Mary Margaret laughed at me when I jumped.

"It ain't nothin' but an ol' polecat. They's more scared of you than you are of them. See 'em all the time around here. Just don't get one of 'em mad at you." I didn't encourage her to talk further about the creatures of the woods, and I looked the other way as we passed old man Braggett's house.

A fire was blazing in the fireplace when we got home. Mary Margaret's father sat whittling in front of the fire. He didn't look up when we came in, but he did stop to spit tobacco juice into the fire. It sizzled where it hit.

Mary Margaret once told me he had a purple heart from the war. "Mama said he ain't never been the same since he got back from that war," Mary Margaret said with a sad look in her eyes. She was born just after her father's return.

I wanted to ask him about the purple heart, but I couldn't quite bring myself to speak to him. Since no one else did, I didn't bother either.

We washed our hands in the tin basin on the back porch and dried them on the flour sack hanging on a nail beside the shelf. I wondered when Mary Margaret's mother had had time to cook, until I sat down, turned over my plate, and took the cold dishes of food as they were passed. I had never eaten cold okra or cold collard greens before, but I supposed if I liked them hot, I would like them cold. The cold chicken reminded me of picnics, and cold mashed potatoes weren't really all that bad once you got them off the spoon.

Mary Margaret and her two younger brothers and I did all the talking. Her mother kept the iced tea glasses filled, and her daddy stared into his plate. But all in all, it turned out to be a rather nice dinner, and I told Mary Margaret's mother so afterward. She acted as though not many people told her they liked her cooking, and she gave me a big hug. "So glad your mama and daddy let you come."

As bedtime rituals go, there were few in that house in the middle of the woods. Mary Margaret's mother had closed the wooden windows for the night and built a fire in the other bedroom where we would be sleeping. We put our jackets on over our nightgowns and started down the path toward the edge of the woods where the outhouse sat in the middle of a little clearing.

"Don't we need a light?" I asked, trying not to sound like a sissy.

"I've got the way memorized. Just foller me." And Mary Margaret took off into the dark, grabbing my hand as she went. I stayed close behind her and wondered about the logistics of going to the bathroom in the dark. I also worried a little about snakes, but with Mary Margaret's natural instincts for finding her way in the dark, we made it safely to and from the outhouse. As we came up the stairs onto the back porch, we splashed our faces with cold water from the wash basin again. I assumed it was the same water we had used at dinner, but it was dark and I couldn't see it so it didn't matter anyhow. We were ready for bed in less than five minutes.

Our bed was in the farthest corner of the room. Mary Margaret didn't say who would sleep in the other double bed. I secretly hoped it would not be her mother and daddy. "Where are your brothers?" I asked as we crawled under the covers. "Probably sittin' out in the bus. Mama don't like their loud music in the house, so they stay out in the bus 'til it gets too cold."

Mrs. Jerkins came in and put more logs on the fire and piled several more quilts on our bed. Since I could already feel a draft from the shuttered windows, I was sure we would need the quilts. "Y'all sleep good now." There was no light, so Mary Margaret's mother didn't have to bother with turning one off on her way out.

We talked for a while in muffled voices under the quilts, since it was too cold to talk above the covers. I got up nerve to ask Mary Margaret if she knew who Douglas Dawes liked, seeing he lived in her community. She didn't know, but she said it could be me. Anyhow, we would see him tomorrow on the bus, and we could ask him then. I decided I really didn't want to know that badly.

"Better get us some sleep. Quarter past five comes awfully early." Mary Margaret was breathing deeply in no time, but I stayed awake for a while and watched the shadows of firelight on boards.

I never did find out who slept in the other bed because I was asleep before anyone came in. But in the morning the covers were pulled back indicating someone had slept there. We dressed in the cold, ate our grits and eggs, and climbed back into the yellow school bus. The sun wasn't even up, and we were on our way to school. We took a different route to avoid walking across the wash so early in the morning. It took us fifteen minutes longer to get to school, but I agreed it was worth it.

Mother was waiting on the front porch when Jimmie

and I got off the bus that evening. "Did you have a good time at Mary Margaret's house?"

I bit into a chocolate chip cookie and answered, "Yes, ma'am." I really meant it. I rehearsed every detail for her, and my brothers sat forward in their chairs, listening with wide eyes. I didn't tell them about "Crazy Man" Braggett and our walk by his house alone at dusk. Maybe sometime when I really wanted to impress my brothers I would tell them. I didn't think Mother and Daddy would be alarmed if they knew, but some things a girl just likes to keep to herself. In fact, thinking about our walk while I sat there in our warm, safe kitchen made me feel quite brave. I was glad Mother and Daddy had let me go home with Mary Margaret, even if it had been a hard decision for them. . . .

Yet even with their example, I struggle to relinquish valuables, to say good-bye. Something within me longs for attachments, permanence, and the status quo. I do not readily welcome the bit of death that occurs inside me with every good-bye. I like my children close by, stable jobs, predictable friendships, and routines that never change.

I work hard to maintain my past, like a craftsman gently restoring some prized antique. I fill our days with tradition and decorate my rooms with family treasures of another day and time. We spend hours pouring over family geneal-ogies and listening to the family lore—storing up riches to pass along to the next generation. But my love of the past, as valuable a pursuit as it is, may also keep me from reaching beyond.

I can never grow through risk until I am ready to welcome change, until I can embrace it not only as a bit of death but also as a bit of rebirth. I must spend a lifetime practicing good-byes, preparing myself for the pain of severance a little at a time. I must release my child to the swimming pool alone for several hours, support a friend who is in the process of moving to another state, and give my husband the freedom to pursue a new job in another location.

In the midst of change, I must provide for familiarity. Some things will not change, and to those things, I must cling. My faith. My family love. Prayers and kisses at bedtime. Candlelight at dinner, something blooming indoors, letters in the mail. They are the stabilities that make change tolerable.

Life is filled with tradeoffs. For every loss, there is gain. I will lose a daughter to a mission radio station in Aruba. But what will she gain through the experience? An opportunity to serve. A view of missions firsthand. An education about another culture. A chance to see how other families live. Opportunities to make decisions on her own.

When it's time for something new, I must willingly let go of the past. I must do as Jesus did. He walked with His disciples, those He loved, out toward Bethany, the place He loved, and there He blessed His past, even as He raised hands of welcome toward the future. He knew it was for their good. "If I do not go away, the Helper will not come to you; but if I depart, I will send Him to you" (John 16:7).

I must be prepared to see those who love me grieve for their loss, as the disciples did, knowing that from this will come growth—courage and conviction. In the disciples' case, growth strong enough to turn the world upside down and launch the new working of God on earth—His church.

I must agree to something new, not necessarily something better. Who could improve on this itinerant instruction in discipleship, direct from the Master's mouth? Perhaps the disciples thought the arrangement would go on forever. But it was time for the new plan. God was not confined in one earthly-divine body to the hills of Galilee and Judea. He was a pulse, a Spirit who moved from person to person, town to town, city to city, and nation to nation. He was everywhere in His people, the church. And it started with a good-bye.

Sometimes I must say good-bye for the greater good. Today I stand at the end of a departure ramp and watch my sixteen-year-old walk alone toward the Eastern DC-10. She is tall and confident in her new pink-and-white outfit, and as I watch her go, I think any mother would be proud. She will be home at the end of six weeks, but I feel the pulling apart just the same, like a shoulder out of its socket, a record needle out of its groove.

This good-bye disrupts the flow. She will not be the same when she returns. I will not be the same. We can never go back. She turns the corner, waves to us, and is gone. Her pink canvas bag is the last thing to disappear. The doors close, the silver bird pulls away from its base. I can do nothing more for her. Severance is complete for a while.

We walk back through the corridors toward the car, but my heart is in a silver bird heading for Aruba. I am with her, yet I am not. It's the pain I will carry with me. But I must risk separation for the sake of growth—my own and my daughter's.

Today, a year removed from her Aruba mission, Jori sits in the middle of a group of four-year-olds—her Sunday school class. A little girl sits crying outside the circle. "Tell me why you're sad," Jori says as she kneels beside her and puts her arm around her. The four-year-old brushes the tears away with the back of her hand. "I . . . I . . ." Her words are stuck between her sobs. "I . . . miss my Sunday school in Texas."

Jori gathers the sobbing child into her arms and holds her close. "It's hard to say good-bye to people we love, isn't it?" The child cries out her grief for a little while, content to sit in Jori's lap. Finally, she straightens her back, looks at Jori with tear-streaked face, and says, "Do you have Play-Doh in this Sunday school?" Within a short time she is happily molding Play-Doh at Jori's table with the rest of the children. But she doesn't leave Jori's side for the rest of the morning.

I don't know what stopped the child's tears, but perhaps she sensed some hidden understanding from her Sunday school teacher who knew what it felt like to be alone in a new situation. Perhaps it all began with a mother who stood wiping her tears on a departure ramp while a silver bird pulled away from the gate and carried her sixteen-year-old thousands of miles away from home.

PART THREE

RISK TAKING

What's in It for Me?

11

One Giant Step to Kansas
Reaping Personal Dividends

Fall has come to Minneapolis, but you can't quite tell it. Summer is hanging on by a thread. The grass is still green, the air warm, the flowers still in bloom, but the calendar reads September 21 and the days are beginning to fade by six in the evening.

We drive around the city block for the third time, partly because we can't find a parking place and partly because we aren't sure what I'm going to do once we reach our destination. We have followed the interstate north, obeyed the big green signs on the overpasses, and made the proper turns. The impressive convention center looms before us. When we find a parking place, we will walk into the edifice that rules over the entire block like the Parthenon, find a registration table, and look for the S's. For me, plans end at that point.

It's the story of my life right now: circling the block with nowhere to go once I find a place to stop. Between seasons—no longer summer, not quite winter. My future is like my presence at this convention; there is no niche for me, no place of belonging, no nametag designating me an official delegate.

There's a nametag for Mark. The church paid the $200 fee for him, and he is in with all the accouterments: a convention packet to call his own, meal tickets, maps and brochures of places to see in Minneapolis. Perhaps even more important is his place of identity: Mark Senter, minister of youth, Arlington Heights Evangelical Free Church.

At the moment, I feel I have no identity. Ruth Senter: person. That's it. No longer student. Not yet professional or mother. Today Ruth Senter, person, doesn't seem enough. I stare up at the massive concrete walls of the convention center. What is there about me to write on a nametag? Nothing. Why should I even go inside? There's no reason.

But I have come all this way. Mark and I have had morning coffee, lunch, afternoon coffee, and dinner together, mixed in with eight hours of conversation as we drove north—a luxury life does not often afford. I'm here on a lark of sorts. Free housing with friends of friends. Free ride north. Nothing to keep me home as I wait for a job to open up.

"You might as well wait in Minneapolis," Mark had said last night. In an hour I was packed and ready to go. To what? I had no idea last night, and today I still have none. We do not have the $200 registration fee. After finishing up my degree and Mark's work at seminary, there's no surplus for extras like conventions.

If the convention center is intimidating from the outside, inside is even more so. People are here because they know where they're going, what they're doing, and where they've been. The registration lines are neat and orderly, divided by first initial of last name. The registrations run into the thousands, and those in charge navigate the conferees with military precision. Colored nametags designate meal times, and numbers in the left-hand corner of the tags signify particular focus and response groups. There's even a color code for transportation to and from hotels. I sense Mark's anticipation as he pins his badge on his sweater and studies the map for the location of his first seminar.

We have thirty minutes before the official convening of the assembly. Since I have no badge, I will not be allowed beyond the banks of double doors that open into the main hall. I look at the map of the city in search of the nearest museum or park. Right now just having a place to go sounds like stability. I study the map and pick my spot— Wallace Art Center, Groveland Avenue. But I'm not enthusiastic. The spot I have picked is just a dot among a tangle of blue lines. There's no meaning to it, just somewhere to go to fill an afternoon. I have no reason to go there, nothing to give or carry away, except pleasure, and pleasure doesn't seem to be what I'm looking for today.

As Mark walks with me toward the outside exit, I see a large conspicuous sign—Press Room. I'm certain it's not for recruitment purposes but to direct those of the elite press corps. A large green arrow points up the stairs.

"Hey, why don't you try the press room? Maybe they need some help." Mark stops by the sign and throws out his ideas as though he is suggesting a walk around the block. I am halfway to the exit before I stop and look back. He is still standing by the green arrow. He isn't kidding. I realize he is prepared to walk up those stairs.

I love the man for his spontaneity and creative impetus, but not when it puts me on the line. He is not the one looking for a place to belong, so it's easy for him to say, "Try the press room." He is not the one setting himself up for rejection. He is not the novice who carries no credentials except aspirations and a meaningless card, given to me during the concluding evening of a writers' conference. Maybe carrying a fake press card helps dreamers take the leap. So far, it hasn't worked for me, and I've carried the card for four months. In fact, I'm not sure why I've even kept it.

I thank Mark kindly for his idea, but suggest it's time to move on. "Let's not pretend," I say as I continue toward the exit.

"How about just a look in the press room?" Mark is merciless in his challenge. "After all, it's not every day you get a chance to peek in on the information hub for a world congress on evangelism."

I agree to look, but nothing more.

We follow the arrow to the third floor. I hear the click of teletype machines and watch as badges with green ribbons flash past me. Important people, on their way to reporting something important. The press room is large and spacious with glass windows that view the main assembly and a network of electronic sophistication: cameras, cables, monitors, a teletype machine, desks, and typewriters. The far end is taken up with press conference furnishings: a long table with chairs drawn up to one side, microphones, and glasses of water. I view it all from the hall with passive indifference—like one who views the Red Room in the White House. A nice place to visit, but I have no illusions of ever belonging there. I'm ready to go. I've seen the press room.

"How badly do you want to be a part of this convention?" Mark does not give up, but today I am not quick to pick up on his challenges. At the moment, I prefer quiet peaceful parks where I can walk in solitude and no one knows whether I fail or succeed. Or museums where I can get lost among the artifacts of history. Surround myself with greatness, then I don't have to meet any challenges for myself. I prefer to ride the city buses and follow the Minneapolis maps. At least I don't have to risk rejection that way.

I stand in the hall, listening to the drone of the teletype and counting the tiles in the floor. I'm caught in a moment of agonizing suspension, as real as the empty spaces a trapeze artist looks out upon when letting go of one trapeze in order to grab the other. I don't think I'm ready to let go and reach for another place. There are too many empty spaces in between. So I stand in the hall and count the tiles. It's fifteen minutes until opening session. . . .

———————————— 🐿 ————————————

I stood one day on the Kansas flatlands and counted clouds as I'm counting tiles today and for much the same reason. As a third grader, I was standing on my own trapeze of sorts, still clutching one, not quite ready to catch hold of the other. We were on our way to Hesston where Daddy would go to college. I counted the clouds that day to pass the time, to fill up the empty spaces in my heart, to forestall the inevitable. The next day I would start third grade without knowing a single person.

The clouds were white, and the sky was very gray. I noticed the sky because it seemed to be all there was to Kansas. It stretched itself overhead like a canopy and then dropped off into the wheatfields beyond. The vast canopy was frightening because I didn't know what was under it. The unrestrained prairie wind blew its cold September breath on us and sent us scurrying for flying napkins and paper plates. It was not a day for picnics, but it was better than unpacking the trailer or eating in the car. Besides, only an hour or two and we would be there.

I squinted my eyes and tried to distinguish what was up ahead, but we were too far from anything. I had to be satisfied with an arrow-straight, two-lane highway, a solitary picnic table by the side of the road, and the restless, rustling fields of forever wheat.

Hesston, Kansas. I'd seen it in my dreams and thought of it day and night for the last six months since Daddy had announced one night at dinner that he and Mother felt God guiding us to Kansas for a while. For me, Kansas might as well have been the moon, except that Kansas had a school where Daddy would finish his college degree and get further training for the ministry.

I had stared hard into my bright yellow dinner plate that night six months ago and struggled to swallow my peas, which kept getting mixed up with the lump in my throat. Kansas. I tried to think of what might be there. For one, my family would be there. Mother. Daddy. Jimmie and Denny. Beyond that, I could not imagine. But if Mother and Daddy thought we should go, I supposed we should go.

Several months after Daddy's dinner-time announcement, he brought home the eighteen-foot house trailer, and Mother started packing away things we would not need for our two-year stay in Kansas. As I watched her, I began packing away my heart. How could I leave my friends? I started collecting their pictures, saving their notes, and stockpiling their love for the bleak Kansas prairies where the wind would blow cold with nothing to stop it. I had looked up Kansas in the encyclopedia, so I knew about the wheatfields. The pictures had been in black and white. There would be no sunshine in Kansas. How can there be sunshine without friends?

All those thoughts went through my mind as I sat by the road and counted the clouds. The encyclopedia had been correct. Kansas was black and white. Kansas was also a new school, classmates I'd never met, snow I'd never experienced, and prairies I'd never lived on. Kansas was a wide empty space of unknowns.

Mother and Daddy didn't know much about our new life in Kansas either. They had been promised a job as resident dorm parents for freshmen men, so we would live in an apartment in the dormitory. Daddy would also work three days a week at the IGA grocery store, pastor a small rural church part-time, and study education and Bible in between. Mother would do laundry for the college students until she had another baby in March. Jimmie and I would walk six blocks to school. Other than that, we didn't know anything about life in Kansas except the sky and wheatfields.

We gathered up the picnic remains, climbed back into the car, and drove on. Several hours later, I spied Hesston, sitting ahead on the edge of the flatland. As we got closer, I could make out the wide trees spreading above the streets. They were not pines, but at least they were trees.

Giant elm trees surrounding the white three-storied dormitory house were the first things I noticed as Daddy backed the trailer into the drive. A green sign hung beside the door: Welcome to the Elms. I thought it was a lovely name, and already I was beginning to feel the block of ice in my stomach melting. The porch was pillared, wide and inviting, and the front oval door was mostly glass. As long as Hesston had a porch and trees, it had some feel of Alabama.

Mealtime seemed like a foreign ritual. We ate on strange dishes. We walked across green-and-gold linoleum instead of Mother's soft braided rugs on the floor. Rather than knotty pine with its cheery warmth, the walls were painted and flowered wallpaper. Even our conversation sounded different in the room with its high ceilings and bare floors. All the world was out of sync. We were living someone else's life, sleeping in someone else's beds, and eating off someone else's dishes. I didn't even feel like me.

But some things never changed. Daddy reached for *The Egermeier's Bible Story Book* and read about Abraham. I forgot the empty prairies and the flowered wallpaper. I was Abraham as surely as if I had been standing in the middle of those brightly colored pictures in the book. We were starting out on a very long journey, not knowing the stopping-off points along the way or where the end would be. We loaded our camels, gathered our caravans in obedience, and headed east and south toward Hebron.

The camels' feet plodded on the baked desert. The sun scorched, and the wind burned with dust. We had every reason to stay in Haran where things were safe and well established. Everyone knew "Terah's boy." We had never organized a caravan or navigated the desert. How would we buy bread? Where would we get firewood? What would our camels drink?

And we did not know about the Canaanites, the Amorites, or the people of Sodom and Gomorrah. What if they didn't like foreign caravans passing through their land? Worse still, what if they laughed, thought we were impostors with our foreign accents? But it was too late to turn back. We had already passed the city limits of our hometown. We were on our way.

That first night I lay awake for a long time, looking out my window on the little trailer, which had come all the way from Brewton, Alabama. The trailer seemed more like home than this room so small that only a bed and dresser fit; this room, more passageway than bedroom. It was the only entrance to our apartment, except the front door where the students came and went. All the rest of the world would come and go through my bedroom. I turned toward the wall and gave way to my tears.

Two years later, I stood proudly beside Daddy in the rose garden of the college, outside the gym. Graduation ceremonies had just ended. Daddy was wearing his blue cap and gown, and he carried a leather-bound diploma in his hand. Mother, Jimmie, Denny, baby Daryl, and I were gathered around, squeezing closer so we could all get into the picture. The roses were brilliant in their display, Mother was soft and cool in a light lavender dress, and I thought Daddy had never looked more handsome. Everywhere we walked, people came up and shook Daddy's hand or gave him a hug. I felt I would burst with pride as I listened to their congratulations.

"You did it the hard way, Elam, but you did it well!"

"Thank you for all you have brought to this place. We will miss you."

"Elam, you did a great piece of work here. Gertrude, you should be proud!"

I watched as Mother brushed away the tears of happiness. I thought I saw the same kind of tears shining in Daddy's eyes, too. He had accomplished the goal of his life, and we were all gathered around him to feel his joy. When the people from the little church in Protection, a small farming town to which we had driven two hundred miles round trip every Sunday, asked Daddy to be their pastor, he thanked them for the high honor but said, "I must return to Alabama to my people." I knew then the cycle had been completed. Daddy's joy was full. He had finished his college education and was going back to Alabama. . . .

Why uproot your family and go all the way to Kansas for two years? Why spend hours on your feet behind a cash register in an IGA grocery store? Why wear out your eyes over books until one in the morning? Why drive four hours every Sunday to preach for a small group of believers? Why more of the lean years when every penny goes to pay a college bill? Why a house with noisy college students and green-and-gold linoleum on the floor? Why a third grader who turned to the wall one night and cried tears of loneliness?

Why Kansas? For the sake of obedience. For the sake of one man's life dedicated to God. For the cotton farmers in the rural communities of southern Alabama and the three little white churches that Daddy built.

But maybe also for the sake of his daughter, who years later stands with indecision outside a press room in Minneapolis, Minnesota. Maybe so that she would have the courage to walk up to a desk, face a man whose nametag bears a name she has read in Christian publications for years, and offer her gifts when she isn't sure she has any to give. Maybe for the sake of that first small job in a press room, maybe for the editor of a Christian magazine who hired her, on the spot, there in the press room. Maybe for the years of writing and editing that came as a result of that venture into a Minneapolis press room—hours sitting behind a typewriter, agonizing over words, pasting copy to a page, thinking up headlines, and cropping pictures so they fit the space. Maybe for the books and magazine articles in print that will somehow contribute to building the kingdom of God.

Why Kansas? Maybe so one daughter will see firsthand the rewards of risk and have the courage to follow.

12

The Preacher Who
Lost His Church
Investing in the Future

Travel posters are the dreams life is made of—tropical
beaches of the Caribbean, ancient cathedrals of Europe,
and quaint cafes along the Riviera. I stop today outside the
travel agency, scan the display before me, and feel the stir-
rings within me. I am here for a Chicago-to-Los Angeles
ticket, but the world beyond beckons. It always has. Each
Sunday when I settle down to read the *Chicago Tribune*, I
turn first to the travel section. I monitor the weather in
Paris or the price of gold in London or read about the *National Geographic* team as it uncovers yet another sunken
treasure in some far-off foreign port.

The silver-haired woman in front of me at the ticket
counter is on her way to a holiday in Australia. She col-
lects her packet of information and asks the agent about

weather conditions when flying over the equator. She has heard they are often turbulent. The ticket agent does not know for sure, but she imagines it has something to do with the hot air that is so intense at the equator. "The airlines know how to cope with weather conditions, even at the equator," she assures her worried client. "And Australia is definitely worth the trip."

I inquire about times and fares to Los Angeles. Traveling to sightsee in Australia is one thing. Scheduling a trip to the West Coast to honor speaking commitments is quite another. I am still trying to decide on the logistics of it all. Do I rent a car in L. A. and drive north or catch a commuter flight and rent a car in Oakland? Should I have someone meet me and drive me to the conference center? Consolidating speaking commitments into one five-day trip has been my way of accommodating my family. This way I will not have to travel again until the end of the year. Right now, I am not sure how accommodating my idea really is or to whom it is accommodating.

The travel agent's fingers fly over her computer keyboard. She wrinkles her forehead, proposes, and counterproposes. This is no small puzzle I have asked her to put together. We finally settle upon a plan, and she agrees to have the tickets ready within a week. I leave, confident about the itinerary but wondering if I could have saved money by flying out of Midway, Chicago's second airport. I decide not to even bother asking.

The skies are clear as I head toward home. The flight pattern from Chicago's O'Hare field is over the western suburbs today, and I can watch the migration of silver birds floating smoothly and effortlessly it seems, restless birds, never content to roost long, always bound for another spot.

Today my spirit feels the same—restless with both feet on the ground. It's one of the strange paradoxes of my life: my passion for one particular plot of earth called home and my love for the open spaces. I don't understand the two parts of me; I don't even try. Life is full of paradoxes, and the sooner I admit to them, the better off I am.

Jori is sitting on the front porch swing waiting for me when I pull into the driveway. She is home early from school. I wonder about the distressed look on her face. Sixth grade has not been her easiest year, and every day seems to bring a new set of emotional vacillations— insecurity to confidence, not-a-care-in-the-world to fear, happiness to sadness, love to hate. Normal symptoms of life's preteen transitions, I say to myself, but still I pay close attention and wonder what is normal.

Mark and I have read the books on parenting, listened to the tapes, talked with parents who are further down the road, and even gathered expertise from our years in youth ministry. But the roller coaster somehow looks higher when you get there yourself.

"Mother." The tears start to flow. "Those girls said they were going to beat me up today after school. I snuck out the back door and ran all the way home." She slumps in the corner of the swing and sobs into her hands.

"Honey, have they hurt you?"

"N . . . n . . . n . . . no."

"Are you okay?"

"N . . . n . . . n . . . no."

Nothing could be more obvious. She is not okay. Her whole body shakes in sobs. I am shaking with her, shaking at the meanness in the world, at the evil of eighth-grade girls who want to beat up a sweet, innocent sixth grader just because they have no better after-school activities.

Why don't they leave her alone? They have vented their hostilities against her long enough.

"I'll call Mr. Greenwalt right away. Those girls have gone a little too far."

"Mother, please don't," she wails. "Then they'll have it in for me because I'm a squealer. They'll call me a baby. Please, Mother, don't."

Her eyes are wide with concern, and I decide that calling the principal is not the course of action to take. Besides, I need time to let my mind catch up with my feelings. I think about life, which transports its children into adulthood without providing cushions for the trip.

Once Jori's sobs have subsided and her fears seemed calmed, at least for now, I suggest an ice-cream bar from the freezer. She is safely home. No eighth-grade bullies have shown up on her doorstep. Mother is near. Now she can move on to ice cream.

I watch Jori bite into the chocolate with nuts. She has all kinds of delicate feelings tucked inside her. Part of her is her mother's daughter. I know how deep little things can go, not to speak of the bigger things like threatening eighth graders who are going to beat you up. Sometimes I wonder if the ill winds in her sixth-grade years will carry us both away.

The ice cream helps for a while but not forever. I am awakened from a deep middle-of-the-night sleep. "Mother, they're coming! Mother, they're coming!"

In an instant I am beside her. She is sitting up in bed, her breath coming in short little spurts as though she has been running. The eighth-grade bullies are out there in the shadows somewhere. I quiet the nightmare, get her a drink of water, and tuck her back under the covers. As Mark and I try to get back to sleep, he mentions that she seems a troubled little girl lately. His words are not the most peaceful of nighttime benedictions.

Jori does not mention the eighth-grade bullies again for several days, but the bounce is gone from her step, and the sparkle is missing from her pretty green eyes. She leaves for school looking as though she has already put in a long, hard day, and she returns like a whipped pup. She is not the Jori we know. We watch, listen, and try to figure it all out.

Even her teacher notices the change and invites me to school for a conference. Mrs. Powell is polite and concerned. There's nothing specific. Jori is obedient. Attentive. Doing what teachers expect from her. Her grades are fine.

"But she seems troubled these days," her teacher says. "Are things stable at home?" she asks almost apologetically.

I am taken aback by the possibility that things might be unstable. I know Mrs. Powell is not prying. She is simply concerned for her student. It's probably good she has asked, for the most unsafe times for my children may actually be when I think they are the safest. During the safe times, I am less vigilant. I think about Mrs. Powell's words, but I also must answer her question.

"Things are stable, yes. It's a very busy time at our house right now, but other than that there's nothing out of the ordinary. I suspect we are just going through a preadolescent stage. This, too, will pass."

Labels are convenient short cuts. I use one today to relieve the guilt I am beginning to feel, as though my busy schedule has indeed been the reason for Jori's dis-ease. Experience has taught me how deadly guilt can be. I am not quick to take on the burden. On the other hand, I am convinced that the atmosphere at home has a direct effect on my child's state of mind. Home is the occasion for good or ill; it does not cause one or the other, it simply feeds, nurtures, and encourages one or the other.

I struggle for balance between the two extremes: "It's just a stage" and "I'm to blame." I know the truth is somewhere in between. I say good-bye to the teacher, express my appreciation for her concern, and walk to the car feeling very unsure about my role as a parent and about the general well-being of my child.

After dinner that night, the conversation between Mark and me centers on my afternoon talk with Mrs. Powell. We will not jump at shadows, we decide, or beat ourselves for our busyness. There are happy children of busy parents and sad children of idle parents; the two are not necessarily related. We will not cancel life because our child is having a tough year. Part of maturity is learning how tough life really can be. Our job is not to see that our child is happy but to see that she is learning about life and about God. We feel satisfied she is progressing in both areas.

Still I go to bed disquieted, resolved I will stop trying to figure out the reasons for Jori's dis-ease and try to concentrate on her needs. I do not have the foggiest idea where to begin. It's a humbling experience.

During the next several weeks I try to concentrate on Jori's needs. Does she need a hug, a listener, a compliment, extra sleep, advice, reassurance? I also start planning ahead for my trip—getting caught up on laundry, grocery shopping, meals, house cleaning, and arranging car pools to and from children's activities when I am gone. Providing for my family's physical needs seems easy in comparison to covering their emotional needs.

"Mother." Jori pushes open the door at exactly 2:34. She has made it from her last class to our front door, a block and a half away, in four minutes. My first thought is the eighth-grade bullies again.

"Mother . . . Mother, you should have heard what the boys said about me in gym today . . ." I can hardly understand her words; they are garbled in emotion. "It was so awful . . . and the whole gym class laughed. I don't have any friends anymore. No one likes me. They are all saying mean things about me . . ." The sobs come in a rush.

She sits on the couch, a pathetic, desolate figure, looking as if all the world has turned her out and she will spend the rest of her days as an outcast. I sit close beside her with our arms touching. She is too big to be cuddled; besides, she isn't the cuddling kind, at least, not for long.

I look down on the sandy head beside me. Bone of my bone. Flesh of my flesh. On loan to me as a gift. Rare. Delicate. Beautiful. So innocent in her trust. So dependent in her pain. So great in her potential. So unpredictable in her needs.

We sit quietly on the sofa for a long time, side by side, not saying anything. Finally, I ask her if I can pray for her. She nods, and we bow our heads together. I wonder which of us feels the more helpless. She stays near me for the rest of the evening, sits at the kitchen counter as I fix dinner, brings her homework into the family room where I am reading the newspaper, and asks me to please come kiss her half an hour before bedtime.

I don't understand the dynamic of what's happening. Jori is not the kind to sit at the kitchen counter and watch me make dinner or bring her homework to the family room just to be close to Mother. She was born tying her own shoestrings, and I'm usually wondering if this independent, self-sufficient child really needs a mother. Today I sense her need, but I'm not sure of the implications for me.

I wonder about parental responsibility. Are there certain emotional needs only a parent can fill if a child is to grow into a productive adult? I think not, since I can name world leaders who grew up without one or both parents: George Washington, Napoleon, Queen Victoria, Golda Meir, and Alexander the Great. I wonder if something in hardship itself nurtures an overcoming spirit. If I bow at the shrine of every emotional need my daughter has, make myself slave to her distressing times, am I doing her a disservice? Another six years and she will be on her own. Am I preparing her for independence by pampering her needs?

My ticket to Los Angeles is on my desk. Just over three weeks until departure. There is something uncomfortable about this red, white, and blue envelope staring at me from atop the "West Coast Trip" folder. It's like a zipper off the track. The elements are not in sync. I have received no obvious message from on high; no Scripture verse convicts me. As far as I know, I do not feel manipulated, guilty, or fearful. But I am not at peace.

I look for logical reasons for my unsettled feelings about the trip. I find none. Jori and Nicky have grown up with parents who travel out of town now and then on ministry. They seem to welcome change in routine when I am gone: Daddy in charge of the cooking, pancake breakfasts in front of the TV, flexible bedtime, Sunday dinner at McDonald's instead of in the dining room with fine china and crystal goblets. I come home to perfect order when Jori is in charge of home management.

"Jori wouldn't let us come in the family room with our

shoes on, and she made us pick up the newspapers and put them out in the garage," Nicky laments when I return. Jori seems to be more competent when Mother is away for a little while. And there is value to space. We all appreciate each other more. I am surrounded by hugging and kissing at the airport when I step off the plane; everyone talks at once. It's always a peaceful departure and a joyful reunion. There are no logical reasons, but I am disquieted just the same. . . .

———————————— 🐚 ————————————

I was disquieted, too, standing there on the wooden dock at Mercer Park as a teen-ager. The Alabama harvest moon cast its shadow on the lake, and the evening was silvery, a moment of outward peace. But inside I felt a jumble of discord. Guilt. Disloyalty. Some dread. Anxiety. Remorse. I had let my mother and daddy down again. I hadn't meant to this time, or the last time, or the time before that. But some decisions a girl must make for herself, especially when she is fifteen. Only this time, I had not been given the option to choose for myself.

"Ruth Ann, you were with your friends all last weekend. We only have missions conference once a year. This Saturday night we'd like you with us at church. We will expect you home in time for dinner."

It had not been an unreasonable request. Special missionary speakers from South America had come to our little church for a week of missions emphasis. I liked the man and his wife. Mr. Brown told hilarious stories, and Mrs. Brown was an accomplished musician. She was teaching me to play hymns on the piano with three-note chords. I was amazed at how much richer the hymns sounded when I used the chords. I had nothing against missions conferences, Mr. and Mrs. Brown, or a mother and daddy who wanted my presence at the Saturday night service.

It was just that the student council sponsored only one picnic a year at Mercer Park. I was the newly elected secretary of the council, and I took my honor seriously. Already I had started to work updating files and had traveled eight hours north to the state student government convention in Huntsville with the new officers.

I also took my job seriously because my current male interest was the president of the council. Brock was not only president, he was Mr. Senior, one of the most popular guys in school. It was easy to take my job seriously with all the attention he gave to his secretary.

When Brock asked me to go to the picnic, it was more than I could do to bring myself to say no—for a missions conference at that! I'd be the laughingstock of the school. It was bad enough that my father was the preacher and gave the invocations at all the graduations and the annual community barbecues, and my parents were the only ones in the whole territory who would not let their daughter date until she was sixteen. There were few Christian kids in our school, and I was not interested in being lumped with a minority—especially a Christian minority. What would it do for my popularity?

When it was time to give Brock my answer about the picnic, I said, "Yes." I tried to say it convincingly. The last thing I wanted was for him or anyone else to know I wasn't allowed to date yet. I had planned the entire afternoon and evening carefully in my mind before he even asked.

The new officers were supposed to spend the afternoon at the home of Ms. Carter, our sponsor, getting ready for the picnic—planning games, buying refreshments, and making signs. It would be easy enough to tell my folks I was going to Ms. Carter's for the afternoon. Brock and I would go to the picnic from there. I would simply not go home for dinner.

I hated to be so obvious with missionary guests staying in our home for the week, but this time I had no choice. I had no choice the last time I lied to them, or the time before that, or the time before that. I was somewhat surprised at how easy it was getting to slip around my parents. It all came from thinking through every angle beforehand. I usually did not miss a detail. As far as everyone at school knew, Brock and I were dating. He thought so, too. I was the only one who knew the difference, and with my acting ability, chances were that I could pull it off indefinitely, as long as I was willing to face the music when I got home. So far it had been worth it. I was "in" at school, and that was all that mattered.

But for some reason, the picnic at Mercer Park lost its flavor as soon as Brock and I got there. I moved through the games with mechanical detachment. I was not where I was meant to be, and I knew it. Even the banana split, my favorite dessert, tasted flat. I ate only three bites and gave away my maraschino cherry instead of collecting everyone else's as I usually did.

Why did the night seem so different? I did not know that back home four adults—Mother, Daddy, and Mr. and Mrs. Brown—were kneeling beside the old brown sofa, praying for me. The Hound of Heaven was in hot pursuit of His wandering child, even though I did not associate my discomfort with His call.

The porch light was on as it usually was when I got home late. From the curve in the road I could also see the light of Mother's white lamp with the pink rose on its base, standing in front of the picture window. Signs of warmth, love, acceptance, and home. They were also signs of judgment to come. I knew my parents well enough to know that they would be waiting for me, and I would have to account for my disobedience. I would not slip off quietly to bed and sleep away my transgression.

"Ruth Ann, we expected you home in time for the evening service. You had given us your word."

I could see the hurt in my father's eyes; he looked tired and gaunt in the dim lamplight. My mother stood in the kitchen doorway, just a few feet behind him. She had taken off her glasses as she got ready for bed, I supposed, and I noticed how black the circles were under her eyes. Part of me wanted to cry, to gather them in my arms and tell them how sorry I was, how much I truly loved them and appreciated all they had done for me. The other part of me would not let go of what mattered most—my friends at school. I had to keep up the front.

"What do you think we should do, Ruth Ann? It doesn't seem to matter to you anymore what your parents think or say. Mother and I have tried to be understanding and reasonable. If we cannot expect obedience from our own child who is fifteen and still living under our roof, we have failed God as parents, and we have failed you." Daddy's voice cracked and I saw the tears gathering in the corners of his eyes. "We just don't know what to do for you anymore."

My daddy was crying over me. It was as bad as any spanking I'd ever gotten. He pulled his big white handkerchief out of the pocket of his robe and cried into it. Long, hard sobs shook his strong, masculine frame while I stood by silently. I didn't want my parents to see the tears in my eyes, so I looked down at the boards in the floor; it was easier than looking into the grief my parents were carrying for me. My mother came, put her arms around me, and cried, too. "We love you, Ruthie. We love you."

Still I stood there looking down at the pine floorboards. Finally, my dad blew his nose and said simply, "You'd better go to bed." Mother turned off the lights, and I walked through the kitchen and turned left into my room, a hollow walk through the place I knew and loved so well. When one is separated in spirit from the other people who live in the home, there is no meaning to the word *home*. I felt the agony of alienation, but for now, it would have to be. I did hope the Browns had not heard my daddy crying.

I was locked into one single passion: to do whatever it took to maintain my "in-ness," protect my image, and keep my friends. Maybe for now it meant my family had to become fixtures—parts of the house, like the big front-room picture window or the braided rugs on the floor—since one does not have strong feelings for fixtures and therefore cannot let them down.

Three months after the Mercer Park episode, our family sat together after dinner while Daddy read the Bible. There around the table sat love while I searched frantically for it elsewhere. There was the thread that kept me connected while I fought desperately for disconnection. I did not know how important the table was. Only the years would tell.

That particular evening, Daddy cleared his throat, the way he always did when he had something important to say. "Mother and I have made a decision. For months we have been praying about it, and now we have our answer. In August we will be moving back to Pennsylvania!" Mother and Daddy had grown up in Pennsylvania. It had been their home for many years, but it was not my home.

The kitchen was suddenly very quiet, as though there was no more time. No future. No friends. No Alabama, place of my heart. I didn't belong in Pennsylvania any more than polar bears belonged at the equator. Alabama was home. Alabama would always be home.

Sometimes when we don't know what else to do, we ask why. Perhaps it's a statement of disbelief, perhaps an attempt to persuade. Perhaps disappointed protest. Why Pennsylvania? The question nagged. It was evident Mother and Daddy loved their work and the people they served. Folks all over the county, and the county next door, knew and loved the preacher who had by now built three churches within a fifty-mile radius. People in little communities with no churches were saying, "Come on up here and start a church for us, too."

People loved the preacher and his wife, and they needed him. If he were gone, who would build the churches and preach the sermons to them? Who would take them firewood when their supply ran low or provide transportation when they had none of their own? Who would lift them out of the ditch when they were so drunk they couldn't find their way home? Who would bury them, marry them, sit with them when they were sick, and comfort them in their loss?

One just doesn't walk out on need. Besides, my dad was not the kind to walk out. Leave Alabama. For what? What would my daddy be if he weren't a preacher? What would our family do if we weren't serving people, inviting them to dinner, taking them hot apple pies, helping them pick their cotton, shelling their butter beans, teaching them Bible lessons, and praying with them? Mother and Daddy had never seemed so happy in their work. The church had never seemed more healthy.

Why Pennsylvania? It didn't make sense, and my mind continued to fight the reality. But letters began to arrive from Pennsylvania, from relatives and friends I didn't even know. Pictures of houses. Maps of the area. Job opportunities. Even several high-school yearbooks so my brothers and I could see what the modern schools looked like in Pennsylvania.

I didn't want a sleek new school with eight hundred students, chemistry labs, and Youth For Christ clubs after school. I wanted my six small classrooms, with initials carved in the desks, glass missing from the windows, and cracks in the cement. I wanted to stay where there were twenty-three students in the sophomore class and where the after-school activities were square dances in the basement under the Future Farmers of America room.

Why Pennsylvania? I was still asking the question when the trucks came for our furniture and our front yard looked like a country auction. I silently cried that question in my tears as folks came from all over the county and the county next door to say their farewells. I asked it as we drove north, as pine gave way to deciduous oak, as red clay disappeared into black topsoil, as warm gulf breezes blew into chilly northern nights, as the southern lowlands changed to hazy mountains and green rolling hills. I asked it even as we crossed the state line. We were into Pennsylvania. We were *not* home.

During the months that followed, I didn't say it in so many words, but I felt it. Why Pennsylvania? I whispered it to God in my loneliness as I slept on the floor in the tiny upstairs bedroom of my grandparents' house while Mother and Daddy looked for a place we could afford. I asked it of the black coal bucket as I shoveled coal into the furnace to heat our three-bedroom duplex when we finally did move. I wondered about it again as we waited for Daddy who was late coming home from his run on the bread truck. His days were long, and he came home walking stiffly after climbing in and out of a truck all day and lifting racks of bread. For the time being, driving the bread truck was the only way to feed his family, even though the driving and lifting hurt his back.

Why Pennsylvania? I never heard my parents ask the question, and they never answered it for me either. They only said, "This is where God has led." I would not understand about the move until years later when I was a parent myself and acquainted with sacrifice, for one cannot recognize sacrifice from another until one has felt its demand on one's life.

Years later, as a young adult, mother of two, sitting by my dad on the green-and-gold sofa of the big, old white house on the hill to which Mother and Daddy had moved fifteen years earlier, I finally found my answer. "Was I the biggest reason you moved back to Pennsylvania?" I asked. Dad looked at me for a long time, as if he was thinking back, remembering that night when the porch light was left on and he and Mother had cried their tears of grief for their fifteen-year-old wandering sheep.

"You were not the only reason." He said it gently with a fatherly protection that had never gone away, even though I was grown, married, and the mother of two. Now I knew sacrifice. Now I could recognize it in another—and receive it from another. I knew I was the reason.

"Thank you, Dad." I put my arms around my father and

hugged him for a long time. I don't remember for sure, but I think we both had tears in our eyes again. . . .

—————————————&————————————

Today I'm still caught in indecision as I stand by my desk and look down at the ticket to Los Angeles. I know what I must do. It does not make sense, canceling out just under a month before I'm scheduled to speak. What about the people on the other end? People who need me. People who are expecting me. What about my future ministry? Will I ever be invited anywhere again? Besides, I have been brought up to keep my commitments. Suddenly I realize, I *am* keeping my commitments.

I go into the kitchen where Jori is eating her breakfast. "Jori, I've decided that this time I'm not going to take my trip. I will stay home with you and Daddy and Nicky."

She is halfway into her bowl of Honey Nut Cheerios. "Why aren't you going?"

I respond with the only answer I have. "This time I feel I need to stay home."

Someday she will understand sacrifice. Meanwhile, she chews happily on her Cheerios and reads the morning comic page. I think, though I am not quite sure, I see some kind of relief on her face. But then, maybe not. She may never say, and I may never know.

Keeping commitments to family is sometimes a risky business because it goes against the trends of the day that make career, advancement, money and reputation seem more important than family. Sacrifice for family is a risk because we never know the outcome. I may sacrifice everything for the sake of my children, and they may go their own way, without care for God or family. But no other risks have greater possibilities for growth in another's life than the risks I take for my children or my husband. Every sacrifice I make for them is leaving an impression of love with them, whether they recognize it or not.

Sacrificing for family is a risk because it means letting go of all the advancements I have heretofore made in my ministry or career and trusting God to continue the progress without me. Sometimes it means obeying Him and trusting that He will ease the inconvenience I may cause fellow workers, supervisors, or people who are depending on my service. Sometimes it means stepping out for the good of my daughter without needing her to understand the sacrifice I have made. Sometimes it means acting on the gentle nudges of the Holy Spirit even when there are no clear-cut reasons. Sometimes it means handing over a career and saying, "It's okay if I never get it back." For risk is not risk until it is willing to lose everything to keep what is most important.

I do not know if canceling a trip to the West Coast for the sake of my daughter made a difference in her life. I do not even know if it was the right thing to do. But until I am willing to look at my family and say, "I love you enough to give up my plans for your progress," I will never see the glory of God in my relationship with them, and even more sadly, they may never see the glory of God in my life. . . .

I see the glory of the Lord, the rewards of risk, here today as I sit at my mother and father's knee, twenty-five years removed from their home. They have known life; they have known pain. It is etched on their faces in lines of strength and courage. Gone are the bread truck and the butcher's block where Daddy cut meat for a while to feed his family. For the last twenty years my parents have served a body of believers in these quiet rolling hills of eastern Pennsylvania where the Susquehanna River threads its way through the foothills of the northern Appalachians. Here in the hospitals and prisons my mother and daddy have walked, held the hands of the sick and dying, taught the Word to those behind iron bars, counseled the depressed and estranged, and ministered hope to unbelievers. Here also they have finished raising their family—four boys and one girl, all now grown and married.

Why Pennsylvania? Only Omniscience, who holds the blueprint, knows for sure. But maybe for all those who are in heaven today, rejoicing around the throne because of my parents' witness here in the foothills of the East. Harvest. Double harvest. Maybe even triple harvest. Rewards of risk. Why Pennsylvania? Maybe for the sake of one daughter. Maybe even for the sake of a book written in tribute to risk.